The World We Create

The World We Create

A Message of Hope for a Planet in Peril

Frances Beinecke

with Bob Deans

Foreword by Sigourney Weaver

ROWMAN & LITTLEFIELD
Lanham • Boulder • New York • London

Published by Rowman & Littlefield
A wholly owned subsidiary of The Rowman & Littlefield Publishing Group, Inc.
4501 Forbes Boulevard, Suite 200, Lanham, Maryland 20706
www.rowman.com

16 Carlisle Street, London W1D 3BT, United Kingdom

British Library Cataloguing in Publication Information Available

Library of Congress Cataloging-in-Publication Data Available

Beinecke, Frances
The world we create : A message of hope for a planet in peril / by Frances Beinecke, with Bob
Deans.
p. cm.
Includes index.
ISBN 978-1-4422-3637-0 (cloth : alk. paper) -- ISBN 978-1-4422-3638-7 (electronic)

∞™ The paper used in this publication meets the minimum requirements of
American National Standard for Information Sciences Permanence of Paper for
Printed Library Materials, ANSI/NISO Z39.48-1992.

Printed in the United States of America

To my three daughters, Carrie, Mary, and Lizzie, who inspire me each day, and to their generation's environmental future.

Contents

Foreword

By Sigourney Weaver

One summer day several decades ago in the Adirondack Mountains, my good friend and neighbor Frances Beinecke dropped by our camp to ask me to help her dismantle the work of some beavers. That may seem an unusual request, but Frances had her reasons. The beavers had erected an imposing dam, stretching twelve feet across the southern end of a wild pond nearby, and the tall pines and cedars along the water's edge were gradually being submerged and beginning to die. If left to stand, the beavers' handiwork would disrupt the entire balance of life in the pond and transform it into a ghostly, sunken forest called a "pughole."

Frances and I arrived and admired the dam. An engineering marvel in native woods, it loomed several feet above the water level, large branches and assorted sticks solidly mortared together with mud. There were two sturdy beaver lodges nearby and a shoreline dotted with freshly gnawed stumps and peeled sticks—sure signs of beavers very much in residence. So, keeping an ear out for the slap of an aggrieved beaver's tail, Frances and I rolled up our sleeves and pant legs and waded in.

It wasn't easy work. We rolled away heavy, wet logs and matted debris, pulling with all our combined might in several directions. Slowly, we were able to dislodge enough mud and matter to start to break apart the dam. When the water finally gushed free, it poured over us in such a deluge that we were literally knocked off our feet. Drenched and laughing, we helped each other up and pared away at the remains of the dam with our bare hands. By the time we finished, the natural flow of the pond had been restored and the water was rapidly draining away from the base of the rescued trees.

I have often thought of that day as I've watched Frances roll up her sleeves and wade into high-stakes debates with corporate polluters and intransigent legislators, grappling to dismantle the rigid systems of prejudice and profit mortared together by these other diligent mammals. The work has been much more daunting than our day at the pond.

For more than four decades, Frances has devoted herself to safeguarding the natural systems that connect each living thing to all the rest in the great web that ties even the smallest among us to the larger world that sustains us all.

Relying on the same natural impulse that led her to save those Adirondack trees, she's risen from an intern to president of the Natural Resources Defense Council, the most effective environmental advocacy group anywhere. We need that advocacy now more than ever because the natural systems we rely on are facing unprecedented threats.

None is more all-encompassing than our addiction to the use of fossil fuels. That dependence is imposing mounting costs on our environment and putting it at needless and growing risk, across our country and around the world. We can wring our collective hands in despair, or we can summon the courage to change. In this book, Frances calls on us to stand up for change. She calls on us to act. More than that, she shows us how. She delivers a message of hope.

There are choices we can make, she tells us, options we can choose, to create a very different kind of future for ourselves and our children. For Frances, it's never been enough to accept the world as it is. It is up to each of us to make our own contribution to leaving this world a better place for our children than what was given to us. That's what this book is all about.

"Standing together, a nation united around the common goals of safeguarding our children's future, reinvigorating the U.S. economy and making our country more secure," she writes, "we can lay out a very different vision of the kind of world we want to create. Then we must unleash the movement required to make it succeed."

Frances and I met in high school, a time when the civil rights movement, the quest for gender equality, and the war in Vietnam taught us that democracy is not a spectator sport. Frances was determined to participate.

It was always clear she was going to be a conservationist. There were many different pathways, though, open to her.

She could have followed in the Rachel Carson mold, writing about the environment and staying clear of the political fray. She might have signed on with a local nature conservancy and left her mark that way.

Instead, she chose a role on the national stage, articulating a vision for a brighter future, laying out a plan for getting there, and then working to make sure her NRDC colleagues have the tools they need to help get it done.

At every step along that journey, she's been opposed by corporate polluters. She's come up against the bitter partisan divisions that have paralyzed our national government on so many levels. And she's struggled to gain the attention of an increasingly distracted public that sometimes appears not to care when, in truth, there are times we just can't bear to look.

Standing up to some of the most profitable and influential industries in history would take its toll on the best of us. Dealing with the U.S. Congress can be frustrating enough to make anyone throw up their hands. And competing for the public's attention in the era of the 140-character twit-bit, the 24-hour news cycle, and the latest fleeting Internet craze can seem like an exercise in abject futility.

Frances, though, has done all of that and managed to stay true to her vision. There just isn't any part of her that knows how to give up. She's remained, through it all, inspirationally optimistic, not only about the goals she has made her life's work but also about the fate of our country writ large.

As an actor, I get to tell stories that explore different issues. I'm still learning, though, from Frances, how to stand and deliver hard truths to skeptics.

Not long ago, I accompanied her on a visit to the U.S. Capitol. We met with members of Congress to discuss the way we're damaging our oceans with the carbon pollution from burning fossil fuels. We met with members who were so adamantly opposed to our point of view that staffers admonished us not to so much as utter the words "climate change" in their presence.

Frances took it in stride. She avoided the phrase and stayed focused instead on the science, the policy, and the law. She defined, in her way, the price we are paying, the damage incurred, and the growing threats our children will face unless we act to minimize those costs and risks. Then, in calm, clear, and compelling terms, she outlined the common-sense steps we must take to begin to turn this around.

She made sure we were heard. She created the opportunity to find common ground and laid the groundwork for future dialogue. And, much as she waded into that Adirondack pond to begin the hard work of dislodging those unwieldy logs, she opened the door for more progress somewhere down the road.

Frances understands the long game. She knows the value of the small gesture and the importance of taking what she can get and building on it, even as she keeps her eye on the greater victory to come.

"Our reliance on fossil fuels has developed over more than a century," she writes. "We won't change that overnight. Transforming our economy, our politics, our very way of life to a lower-carbon model is going to take systemic change. It will be the work not of just one generation, but several. In many ways, we've only begun."

As a child growing up camping out in the Adirondack wilderness, I roamed towering forests and hiked majestic mountains as wild and open as all of life seemed to me. I saw the natural Earth as both welcoming and immense, a vast place of no limits and inexhaustible resources. Our planet, though, is far more finite than any of us might once have believed. Its resources are precious. They are the stuff of life. It is on us to safeguard this still magical and wondrous place for the generations to come, to stand up to those who would squander their future for the sake of polluter profits today.

In this book, Frances reminds us that we are at our best when we stay focused and move forward, by making one good decision at a time. Let's make one good decision today, each of us, to help protect our fellow species, our waters, our lands, and our air. And let's do it again tomorrow, and the day after that, until, working together, one generation down to the next, we restore and safeguard our planet Earth.

Acknowledgments

This project was one requiring fast delivery, and tremendous thanks are owed to my primary partner and inspiration for this book, Bob Deans. We traveled together in the Gulf of Mexico after the Deepwater Horizon oil spill and have conferred on a continuing basis over the past four years about how best to communicate the danger of fossil fuel dependence and the urgency of climate action. This book is a result of our travels together and apart to bear witness to what fossil fuel development has meant to people and communities across our country. Emily Cousins, who knows my voice more than any other, I thank for her support, advice, and quick edits! And many thanks go to my other co-conspirators in this project, Lisa Benenson and Willa Bugnon, for ensuring we stuck to the program, focused on the essential, and got the job done!

I am ever grateful to all my colleagues at NRDC who, over many years, have educated me throughout on the details of innumerable environmental threats and prepared me well for the climate fight that must be won. The unwavering vision of John Adams, which has flowed down throughout the entire staff, has propelled all of us over the decades. Peter Lehner has worked with me every day to hone NRDC's advocacy and to focus our priorities. Our climate team, led by David Hawkins, David Doniger, and until very recently, Dan Lashof, has shaped our climate strategy with diligence and tenacity over the decades. It has been my privilege to be part of their team.

Many thanks to my colleagues who have brought into focus the deleterious effects of our fossil fuel addiction; our lands advocates, Sharon Buccino, Amy Mall, and Kate Sinding, who first alerted me to the impacts of fracking; our international specialists Susan Casey-Lefkowitz and Liz Barrett Brown for ensuring I saw firsthand the tar sands destruction in northern Alberta; our oceans champions, Sarah Chasis and Lisa Speer, with whom I have worked side by side to avert the worst effects of offshore drilling in the Atlantic and the Arctic Oceans, and to our public health experts led by Linda Greer, who never let me forget that in the end, or the beginning, it is all about human well-being. I am also grateful to Niel Lawrence and Chuck Clusen for keeping the vision of what a protected Arctic could be in the forefront of my mind at all times. And to Jacob Scherr who accompanied me to Bali, Beijing, and Copenhagen, where we got a close-up look into the complexity of international climate negotiations

There is no strategy without solutions, and Ralph Cavanagh, David Goldstein, and Ashok Gupta have inspired all of us to understand the central role that energy efficiency must play in a clean energy future. NRDC's broad-based energy experts have delved into shaping the policies that will carry clean energy solutions forward. Kit Kennedy, who has joined me on various excursions to see clean and dirty energy projects, has been key to synthesizing NRDC's position on how to make the necessary shifts in America's energy system. In the end, politics are essential to policy solutions, and the trusted advice of Wesley Warren and David Goldston has been central to forming our strategy. NRDC's Board of Trustees has provided me with unending support, and my two Board chairmen, Frederick A. O. Schwarz and Dan Tishman, have provided essential counsel along the way. My thanks go to trustees Patricia Bauman and Tom Roush for traveling with me to see fracking and mountain-top removal firsthand; and to Bob Epstein and Nicole Lederer for assembling hundreds of business leaders into a potent force for clean energy and climate solutions called Environmental Entrepreneurs. And I am grateful to Abby Schaefer for working with me to make NRDC's board one of the most effective and influential in the field.

Particular thanks to Adrianna Quintero and Al Huang and their colleagues within NRDC and outside as we work to develop stronger partnerships across communities of color. Together we can help these communities reduce the disproportionate impact of fossil fuel development and work to create a strong force for climate action.

The threat of climate change requires us to consider the future, and as I weigh the possible outcomes, I am inspired by the young people at NRDC. From recently graduated litigators to community activists to youth bloggers, these staffers have demonstrated their dedication and drive to move American down a more sustainable path. We are fortunate to have this next generation of environmental leaders.

No single organization wages a fight on its own, and the environmental community has legions of folks who have answered the call for climate action. My closest colleagues in this ongoing challenge have been Margie Alt, Gene Karpinski, Fred Krupp, Mike Brune, Kevin Knobloch, George Rakis, Kathleen Welch, Larry Schweiger, and John Podesta when at the Center for American Progress. For inspiration and the drive to reach ever farther, I bow to Gus Speth and Bill McKibben.

The National Commission on the BP Deepwater Horizon Oil Spill and Offshore Oil Drilling afforded me the opportunity to witness up-close the consequences of America's oil addiction, and to focus on addressing the worst impacts of the oil spill and preventing it from happening again. I am grateful to my co-commissioners: co-chairmen Bob Graham and Bill Reilly, and fellow members, Don Boesch, Terry Garcia, Cherry Murray, and Fran Ulmer for the collegial spirit and determination to get to the heart of the matter. We couldn't have done that without the leadership of our executive director Richard Lazarus and the terrifically talented staff that was assembled almost overnight. And my personal appreciation to NRDC's own Ben Longstreth, who joined me on the other side of the firewall during my stint on the Commission.

Several federal agencies have the responsibility to shield the public from environmental threats, including the topic of this book: climate change. We at NRDC have advocated for agencies to adopt smart policies, and we have also used hard-hitting litigation to spur action. Always, I remain grateful to those who carry out the government's obligation to protect public health and the environment, most notably at the Environmental Protection Agency, the Department of Energy, and within the White House. With their dedication, careful analysis, and commitment they are helping to address this critical issue through President Obama's Climate Action Plan. Carol Browner, Heather Zichal, and Lisa Jackson all provided important leadership to reach this point while in the government.

Environmentalists and government officials cannot tackle the climate threat ourselves. We need people of all walks of life to raise their voices and demand action. That is why I am grateful to the millions of people who take time out of their lives to write lawmakers, join marches, speak at town halls, rally school groups and religious communities, and do countless other things that create the momentum for positive change.

I could not have dedicated my life to building a sustainable future if it had not been for the constant support of my husband, Paul Elston, and our three daughters Carrie, Mary, and Lizzie. Despite many missed dinners and all-too-frequent trips away from home, they have been my most stalwart supporters and greatest champions.

Introduction

The modern environmental movement exists for one purpose. We are here to change the world, to create a place where our environment is treated as the single most important physical asset we share, because that's exactly what it is. That's when we'll begin to care for the natural systems of the Earth as if our very lives depended on them, because they do. That is not yet the world we live in. It is the world we must create.

For more than four decades, I have stood on the front lines of environmental advocacy, speaking out for the commonsense safeguards we need to protect our natural inheritance and health. Never, in my lifetime, have the challenges been greater than those we face from climate change. Never have the solutions been more clearly at hand. And never have we had more to gain from taking action today to avert deepening climate crisis tomorrow.

This book lays bare the price we are paying and the risks we are facing to support our costly and environmentally catastrophic addiction to oil, gas, and coal. It sets forth a vision for a more hopeful future. And it concludes with a road map to take us there.

We can reduce the environmental costs and mounting risks of producing these dirty fossil fuels. We can clean up the pollution from burning them. We can invest in efficiency so we can do more with less waste. And we can build wind, solar, and other sources of cleaner, safer, more sustainable power to cut our reliance on these destructive fuels. It is clear that we need to do so.

Standing in opposition to the work we must do are some of the wealthiest and most powerful industries in the world. The stakes, for these industries, are enormous, because we have made it so, through our continued dependence on the fuels they provide.

Right now, in this country, every single day, eight cents of every dollar we spend goes to pay for oil, gas, and coal. Reducing our reliance on these dead-end fuels and the exorbitant toll they exact will put money back in the pockets of our people. It will lay the groundwork for entire new industries and clean jobs that hold the key to global prosperity for generations to come. And it will strike a blow against the single greatest environmental challenge of our time, the widening scourge of climate change.

We've relied for two centuries on fossil fuels in this country. We won't change that overnight, but we have already begun to make the shift. The dramatic expansion of clean and renewable power in the past several years is one of the most encouraging signs I have seen in the climate fight. But much more needs to be done. Over time, we must leave behind the dirty fuels of the past and embrace the great clean-energy promise of the future. That's what being an energy superpower is going to look like as we move further beyond the last century and into the next.

We've made a strong beginning, but this is no time to rest. Not when a deepwater blowout can kill 11 workers and gush 170 million gallons of toxic crude oil into the Gulf of Mexico. Not when ancient mountains are dynamited to rubble and native streams are buried beneath the scree to get to a single seam of coal. Not when fracking and explosive fuel trains have brought the perils and pollution of the oil patch smack in the middle of the American backyard. And not when the dangerous carbon pollution from burning those fuels is wreaking havoc with the global climate system, imposing mounting costs on our communities and putting our people and the natural systems that support us at grave and growing risk.

From the time I was an intern at the Natural Resources Defense Council to the day I became its president, I have always believed that identifying a problem is the first essential step toward change. Step two is to develop a solution, a deliberate and positive course that will solve the problem, mitigate its impact, or stem its advance while we search for the way to turn it around for good. The third step is always to build the national demand for needed change, strengthen the momentum for progress, and summon our collective will to act.

The fossil fuel industry commands outsize sway over our politics, our markets, our commercial media, and, indeed, our system of democracy. We must stand taller still, because that's what this moment requires.

We must tell the truth about what's happening to our environment, based on the best evidence sound science reveals. We must develop the policy solutions we need, engaging all the innovative and creative spirit of our times. We must build coalitions, forge common ground with a widening and increasingly diverse group of allies, and speak with a clear and compelling voice.

This chorus for action is our most potent force. I have learned in my many years as an environmental advocate that the only way to counter the money and influence of the fossil fuel industry is to galvanize public opinion to the point where people across the nation and from every walk of life call on elected officials and demand change. Right now that call is getting louder, broader, and more urgent. None of that will ensure a smooth road ahead or guarantee timely success. It will, though, put us squarely where we need to be, speaking out on behalf of what's best for our future, no matter how long the odds. With an engaged public, we can create the political will for climate solutions and clean energy progress.

Time and again, I have seen this exercise in democracy work: when people call for environmental protection with clarity and persistence, we prevail. That's how we got lead out of our gasoline, cleaned up industrial pollution from our waters, and achieved many other important gains. The fight against climate change will require even greater tenacity.

Through our continuing addiction to fossil fuels, we are courting environmental calamity. And yet, I'm convinced we've arrived at a moment of hope. President Obama has issued a climate action plan that is a challenge for the country to meet. We have a growing community of business and labor leaders, farmers, faith leaders, and others who see the opportunity. And we have a new generation of activists who grasp the urgent need for change.

As we, as a nation, fully embrace the stakes, opportunity, and urgency for change, we'll begin to put a premium on protecting fresh air, clean water, and healthy lands, rather than treating them as expendable resources to be exploited for short-term profit and gain. We'll affirm through our habits, policies, and laws the vital connection between human survival and environmental health, between the quality of our environment and the quality of life we all seek. We will recognize a sound environment as an essential cornerstone of national prosperity and economic wealth, so that we can build for our children a sustainable future of promise and hope.

That is when we will know what it means to treat our environment as the single most important physical asset we share, because that is exactly what it is. That is when we will care for our natural systems as if our lives depended upon them, because they do. That is not yet the world we live in. It is the world we must create.

August 2014, Long Lake, New York

ONE

Our Moment

It was a sweltering afternoon in June 2013 when I arrived at George-town University in the nation's capital and took my seat in the Dahlgren Quadrangle. But I didn't mind the blistering sun: I had waited decades for this moment. The President of the United States had come to announce a concrete plan to tackle global climate change, the central environmental challenge of our time.

From the podium, President Obama said we have an obligation to protect future generations from the dangers of this widening crisis. Those perils, he told us, were unfolding right before our eyes, in powerful storms swamping our communities, in prolonged drought baking large swaths of our nation, and in dirty air triggering asthma attacks in our children. To combat these threats, he laid out what he called his Climate Action Plan, a comprehensive blue-print for change that would touch every corner of the United States.

"As a president, as a father and as an American, I am here to say we need to act," he vowed to students gathered there. "I refuse to condemn your generation and future generations to a planet that's beyond fixing."

It was a thrilling declaration from the leader of the most power-ful nation on Earth—one that, for me, had been a long time coming. For the past two decades, as the executive director, and then presi-dent of the Natural Resources Defense Council (NRDC), I had worked with scientists, public health experts, businesspeople, relig-ious groups, and other environmental leaders to advocate for cli-mate action at every possible level—from state houses to Capitol

Hill, community groups to corner offices, Beijing to Copenhagen. It had been a journey of significant victories and deflating setbacks. We were heartened in 2006, for instance, when California passed the first law to reduce climate change pollution from the electricity and transportation sectors. But in 2010, the Senate failed to take up comprehensive clean energy and climate legislation that had passed in the House of Representatives the year before. Congress became ever more gridlocked, and conventional wisdom held that America would not act on climate change for years to come.

The President's speech was proof to the contrary. In 2012, NRDC policy experts demonstrated through a series of reports and analyses that the Clean Air Act could be used to cut carbon pollution from power plants. As the government began developing an approach to reduce emissions from the electric power sector, the environmental community spotlighted the booming growth of wind and solar power and the vast potential for energy efficiency, while encouraging people across the nation to raise their voices and demand climate action.

That day at Georgetown, President Obama confirmed that he had heard the message. The plan he announced will move our nation down the path toward a clean energy future and a more stable climate. It will require a sustained commitment to get there: Breaking our 150-year-old dependence on dirty fossil fuels will take decades to achieve. But the president's declaration was a start—and the Climate Action Plan quickly began sparking changes across our economy and in our daily lives, underscoring to people everywhere the ways that using efficient appliances and installing solar panels can have a real impact on climate change. As the plan takes hold in American law and life, it will unleash enormous rewards—cleaner air, more jobs, new innovations, economic prosperity.

The Climate Action Plan isn't perfect, and there is more to be done. But it is a signal of hope for those living on the frontlines of climate change: For the residents of New Orleans' Ninth Ward who suffered the blows of Hurricane Katrina; for the Midwestern farmers who struggle through extreme cycles of drought and floods; for the mayors of Southeastern coastal towns who try to shield their communities from sea-level rise; for the Colorado families who lost homes in devastating wildfires; and for all of us who have been fighting for real action on this defining issue of our age.

A PASSION FOR THE WILD

I started my career as an advocate of sustainable land use practices, far afield of the topics of energy use and climate change. But within a few years, the terrible risk that the unfettered use of fossil fuels poses to our planet became clear to me. The more I learned about the looming threat of climate change, though, the more I realized it endangered all the natural systems we depend upon. It's already imposing grievous and growing human consequences, starting with the poorest and least able to cope.

Like so many people, my concern for the environment grew out of my love of wild and beautiful places. I was seven years old in the summer of 1957, when my family journeyed from our home in Summit, New Jersey, to a ranch on the Snake River just south of Yellowstone National Park.

And what an adventure we had, riding horses along winding trails and swimming in bracing mountain lakes, the Grand Teton Mountains rising behind every view. We waded barefoot into cold streams swollen with snowmelt. We wandered through meadows gone to riot with the brilliant yellows, violets, and reds of wildflowers with names like ladies tresses, ox-eye daisy, fairy slipper, and Indian paintbrush. We saw peregrine falcons soar across a sky of crystalline blue. And we watched young antelope learning to run along rolling hills of shale.

From any place on the ranch, the view was iconically American, an Ansel Adams photograph come to life. And everywhere, it seemed, was the powerful and pungent scent of sage, wafting up from grass spread out like a faded carpet of green across broad valleys scraped smooth in the last glacial age.

I didn't understand or even realize it, of course, but something happened to me that summer, something lasting and profound. I had made a connection to the magic unfolding in the natural systems that shape our world. It was vivid. It was personal. And it created a passion for the wild that has directed much of my life.

In the summer following the seventh grade, I journeyed back out west for camp in Kelly, Wyoming. The experience rekindled my childhood memories and reinforced the power of the western landscape on my imagination. The power of that experience stayed with me for the next decade as I wound my way through school.

The America of my high school years was a place of ferment and change. The civil rights movement was in full flower. We were beginning to wage a costly and divisive war in Vietnam. The National Organization for Women was created. Our culture was being recast by music that created a sound to match the times—Bob Dylan, the Beatles, Marvin Gaye, the Rolling Stones.

In the spring of 1967, I attended a talk by the Rev. Jack Russell, one of the most inspiring people I'd ever heard. A Methodist preacher, Russell was with the Boston Redevelopment Authority, and he spoke with passion about the condition of our inner cities and the urgent need to resuscitate them. I spent that summer as an intern with Russell's group, renovating buildings in South Boston, alongside other interns, volunteers, and staff, an intentional mix of young people from the inner city and small towns. I came face-to-face with complex urban and societal issues. It was an eye-opening experience for a private school girl from a town of fewer than 20,000 suburbanites. Those months anchored my growing awareness of the value of public interest work, although at the time I had no real inkling of where that might carry me.

I entered the University of Pennsylvania in the heart of West Philadelphia in the fall of 1967. Students and faculty at Penn sponsored "teach-ins" meant to inform the students on the war in Vietnam. That fall 50,000 people marched on Washington to protest the escalating war. The next few months would bring the assassinations of Dr. Martin Luther King and Robert Kennedy and unleash a wave of grief, confusion and national soul searching.

One of the most divisive years in our country's history, 1968, ended with a moment that pulled the nation together. On Christmas Eve, the three-man crew of *Apollo 8* became the first manned mission to orbit the moon, preparation for the flight that would put the first men on the lunar surface the following year. The astronauts beamed back a Christmas message, reading from the book of Genesis. Then, as a parting gift of the season, the crew sent home one thing more, something no one in history had ever seen before: a photograph of Earth, its waters and dry land, rising beyond the vast and desolate surface of the moon, a dazzling blue and white jewel adrift in the dark and infinite void. We had seen satellite photos of parts of the planet, but we hadn't seen it whole and alone in space before this. The picture was called *Earthrise*, and the late nature photographer Galen Rowell called it "the most influential environmental photograph ever taken."

The poet Archibald MacLeish put its meaning into words, writing in *The New York Times*: "For the first time in all of time men have seen the earth: seen it not as continents or oceans from the little distance of a hundred miles or two or three, but seen it from the depths of space; seen it whole and round and beautiful and small."

A CLASS OF OUR OWN

My years at the University of Pennsylvania opened my eyes to the turmoil embroiling our nation. It put me in the company of students and professors who were socially and politically engaged. It challenged me to find my place in a progressive movement that was taking shape around critical issues too long ignored. Like many if not most college students of that era, I was overwhelmed by what felt to me like some seething cauldron of upheaval and change. It rocked my sense of security. Then, in the spring of 1969, Yale University announced it would admit women as undergraduates for the first time since its founding in 1701. Once every 268 years, I figured, a chance like this comes along. I wanted to be part of it.

That fall I entered Yale University as a transfer student, a member of the first class of women in the school's history. We knew there were high expectations for us from both outside and within the University—but those expectations were no greater than the hopes we had for ourselves. We had been given a tremendous opportunity; how would we use it? What could we achieve?

As the currents of social change coursed through the life of the nation, there was a mounting awareness of the damage we were doing to our environment and health as the result of our industrial practices, our growing culture of consumerism, and our overall way of life.

In January of 1969, an oil well blew out off the coast of Santa Barbara, sending four million gallons of toxic crude oil into the Pacific Ocean and coating some of the most beautiful beaches in southern California with a tar-black sludge. It contaminated marine habitat and killed birds and fish in a disaster that President Nixon said "touched the conscience of the American people."

"What is involved is something much bigger than Santa Barbara," he said after flying over the area to see the damage first hand. "What is involved is the use of our resources of the sea and the land in a more effective way and with more concern for preserving the beauty and the natural resources that are so important to any kind of society that we want for the future."

"I don't think we have paid enough attention to this," Nixon continued. "All of us believe that, all of us who have watched America grow as it has grown so explosively since World War II."

Instead of paying attention, we were paying a high and mounting environmental and public health price for our nation's soaring growth. In the industrial heartland rivers, ran so thick with chemical pollution they literally caught fire. Los Angeles was declared the world capital of smog. Forests were dying from acid rain. Our cars were belching lead into the air we breathe. And the federal and state governments were not organized to take a reasoned and systematic view of how best to protect the natural systems we depend upon, or even to inventory the damage we were doing to those resources.

"AN ENVIRONMENT OF DECENCY . . . "

Across the country, community groups were searching for ways to harness environmental concerns to the social activism fueled by the movements around civil rights, women's liberation, and the war in Vietnam. Inspired by the momentum of those movements, U.S. Senator Gaylord Nelson and community activist Denis Hayes came up with the idea of a single day of organized events aimed at informing the public about environmental damage and threats and the need for national action and change.

Nelson, a Democrat from Wisconsin, wrote letters to the mayors of major cities and the governors of all 50 states asking them to proclaim April 22 as what he called Earth Day. He helped raise money for the event, while Hayes, who grew up in Washington State, helped rally state and local groups to the cause. Nelson penned an editorial declaring: "Earth Day is a commitment to make life better, not just bigger and faster. It is a day to reexamine the ethic of individual progress at mankind's expense."

The initiative was more successful that anyone had imagined.

On April 22, 1970, some 20 million Americans turned out for teach-ins, speeches, demonstrations, and other community-based events designed to celebrate the first Earth Day, in what *The New York Times* would later call "among the most participatory political actions in the nation's history."

At Yale, the event was headlined by U.S. Senator Edward Kennedy, a Massachusetts Democrat and the younger brother of two slain leaders: U.S. Senator Robert F. Kennedy and President John F. Kennedy. He spoke about the need for environmental stewardship.

Yale was immersed in a university-wide strike to protest the up-coming trial in New Haven of Bobby Seale, co-founder of the Black Panther Party, which fought police brutality and advocated for bet-ter social conditions for the African American community. Seale was charged with conspiracy in the murder and kidnapping of a fellow Black Panther. On campus, we regarded the trial—which ended more than six months later in a hung jury—as a farce and an affront to a civil rights leader. On a day when thousands of stu-dents, myself included, staged a campus-wide strike, Earth Day was not the focus, though social justice and the need to be an engaged citizen were.

I didn't consider myself much of an environmentalist in the early 1970s—the environment was one of the many issues concerning my generation of college activists. But I was spending more time in the natural world, hiking in the White Mountains of New Hampshire and the Adirondack Mountains of New York. I was connecting more deeply on a personal level with the landscapes that had in-spired people for generations. I joined the Sierra Club at the sugges-tion of my dear friend Sarah Bates, and I began to feel the link between these beautiful places and the activism swirling all around me.

Within months, Nixon and Congress established the Environ-mental Protection Agency. It was jarring to see a president who was largely reviled on college campuses become a champion for envi-ronmental safeguards, but we welcomed his leadership in that area all the same. By year's end, Congress passed—with overwhelming bipartisan support in both houses of Congress—and Nixon signed the Clean Air Act. Over the next two years, Congress added the Clean Water Act, the Coastal Zone Management Act, the Marine Mammal Protection Act, and other bedrock environmental legisla-tion reflecting a broad, bipartisan national consensus for protecting our natural systems.

Earth Day was a turning point in the development of the envi-ronmental movement. It was a grass-roots phenomenon that helped galvanize national interest in protecting our waters, lands, wildlife, and air. Citizen action focused political firepower on the need for laws to prevent unchecked pollution, providing impetus for some of our most important environmental laws. And it pulled the coun-try together around the idea that we have an obligation to leave our environment—at home and abroad—in better shape for our chil-dren than our parents left for us.

I often think back on college as my full-fledged baptism into activism rather than academics. At Yale much of our time was spent focused on politics, the arrival of the National Guard on campus, the civil rights and anti-war movements engulfing the country. Something remarkable was happening. All over the country, people were on their feet and demanding change. The way we were treating our people, and the people of other lands, and the way we were treating the world's natural systems all seemed to be blowing up in our face. And students everywhere were standing up and speaking out to say: Enough.

In the few short years since high school, I had undergone an awakening. I'd encountered the challenges of my time: urban ills, racial inequity, gender discrimination, a festering war, and degradation of our environment. I'd learned that democracy is not a spectator sport, but a participatory process that belongs to those who are willing to show up, knock on doors, raise their voices, and take it to the streets. I'd seen the promise of progress imbedded in real change forced by the conscience of a vigilant nation. In June of 1971, I donned my cap and gown as part of the first class of women to graduate from Yale University.

SLOW BOAT TO BUKAVU

That summer my close friend Lucie Sides and I traveled to East Africa to take a breather, explore a different part of the world, and consider the direction we wanted to take in the future. We traveled through East Africa, exploring Kenya, Tanzania, Uganda, Rwanda, and the Congo, visiting Peace Corps volunteers and seeing friends of friends along the way.

I was mesmerized by the natural riches of the vast Serengeti, its sweeping savannah grasses and acacia trees, the morning sunlight on a herd of zebra, the sounds of hyenas on the hunt by the darkness of night. It was illuminating: the landscape, the wildlife, increasing populations of the cities, and the growing conflict between the natural world and human needs.

I was 21 years old. It was my first visit anywhere in the developing world. I had witnessed urban poverty in the United States, working in South Boston. This, though, was something different—a view to what poverty means in a place where the starting point is a scramble for basic survival, particularly for the most vulnerable among us—the children, the elderly, and the poorest of the poor. I talked to women who walked for miles every day to collect water and firewood. Idi Amin, Mobutu Sese Seko, and other strongmen ruled over much of the region, adding the threat of political violence to the struggles of providing food and shelter for loved ones. Rwanda one of the most densely populated countries in Sub-Saharan Africa, a place where competition for land is keen. Deforestation of the volcanic slopes was visible to us as we watched women trudge back and forth to haul water and collect firewood.

I left Africa a different person, inspired by its people and places, shaken by the distance between my stable and peaceful life and the challenges faced by millions of others. We had wandered, almost carelessly, through a collection of young nations struggling to break free of their colonial pasts. We had little idea of the conflicts already developing, the unspeakable horror and incomprehensible heartbreak yet to unfold across many of the places we visited.

I have thought back to this trip many times over the years—the opportunities and challenges that we saw stretching out before a new generation of post-colonial Africans. The experience left an indelible impression, alerting me to unbreakable ties between the health of the environment and the well-being of people all over the world. I learned, in those months, something about the power each of us has to make a difference in our communities and the larger world, and the responsibility we have to make the best of that. The question for me was, How?

"FOREVER WILD"

The natural world was taking hold of me as I contemplated career paths. Upon my return from Africa, I spent the fall auditing classes at Yale and camping in the great forests of northern New York, the Adirondack Mountains.

The product of more than a billion years of volcanic eruptions, ocean sediments up to 15 miles deep, tectonic uplift, erosion, and glacial carving, the Adirondacks rise up over upstate New York between Albany and the Canadian border.

In one of the most assertive conservation measures in U.S. history, New York set aside its state lands in the Adirondack and Catskill mountains in 1885, declaring the areas "forever wild." State-owned wild lands in the Adirondacks now total nearly three million acres. Separately, in 1892, the state created the Adirondack Park, a distinctly unique park incorporating both public and privately held lands. During the 1970s, the 3.4 million acres of privately held land in the park became subject to conservation covenants, preservation provisions, and state-of-the-art land use controls. The result is a wilderness park with a total of nearly six million protected acres. That's roughly the size of Vermont, and it's larger than the national parks at the Everglades, Yellowstone, and Grand Canyon—combined.

In the late 1960s my family bought a forested parcel beside Long Lake, one of more than 3,000 lakes and 30,000 miles of rivers and streams in the Adirondacks. Long Lake drained north, down the Raquette River and into the St. Lawrence River. And on the other side of the divide, the eastern Adirondacks provided the primary watershed and the headwaters of the Hudson, long the centerpiece of environmental activism in New York state. The Adirondack Mountains appeal to people who like untamed places. The state and numerous advocacy organizations over the years have worked hard to ensure that its natural systems, its beauty, its inherent wildness is protected. The need for vigilance to protect this landscape is ongoing. It was here I found a mixture of the nature that inspired me and the activism that would be needed to ensure its future.

That discovery helped inspire me to enroll in the Yale School of Forestry and Environmental Studies that fall. One of the oldest institutions of its type in the country, the school was co-founded by Gifford Pinchot in 1900 to bring forest management to the United States. Pinchot, who helped create the U.S. Forest Service, was, in many ways, the conscience behind President Theodore Roosevelt's extraordinary commitment to protecting American wild places from reckless industrialization and exploitation and to creating wildlife refuges and the National Forest system, ensuring that America had a conservation mandate even as the resource extraction industries were at their strongest.

By the time of my arrival in the early 1970s, the school had become a hotbed of environmental leadership and an incubator for fledgling talent. Forestry had taken a back seat to resource management, environmental awareness, and the preservation of our natural world. It was a line of study that seemed to me the culmination of what my life had been arcing toward since that first scent of sage I'd experienced as a seven-year-old in the wilds of Wyoming.

In the summer of 1973, midway through my two-year masters' program at the forestry school, I got an internship that would change my life—at the Natural Resources Defense Council. In those days, NRDC was a fledgling and chronically short-staffed group of environmental attorneys. Led by the charismatic and visionary executive director John Adams, the organization was operating on a shoestring. Some days it wasn't clear who would answer the phones. But they were serious about their mission. In the contest between polluters and a healthy environment, they believed, someone needed to stand up for nature. The NRDC team in those early years defined environmental advocacy—the use of law to hold polluters to account, and to make the government, the EPA, the Forest Service, the Interior Department and others do its job.

Few, if any, of us take a job out of school expecting to stay for the next four decades. Certainly that wasn't on my mind when I joined NRDC that long ago summer. And yet, four decades later, here I am. Over those years, the work I was asked to do, the issues that arose for us, the colleagues I collaborated with, and the things we accomplished reminded me every day that I was in the very best place possible to be to advocate for environmental protection.

TANGLING WITH THE FOSSIL FUEL INDUSTRY

The work grabbed me right from the start. John Adams believed firmly in pulling new staffers into meaty projects. He was an extraordinary mentor to me and to legions of environmental advocates over the years. His sense of what is right never wavers, and his client is first and foremost the natural world. As soon as I came on board, John gave me meaningful work to dive into. I began by helping propose a land use plan for New York state's Catskill Mountains. Then Congress passed the Coastal Zone Management Act in 1974, and along with my close colleague Sarah Chasis, we helped make sure the law was enforced in a way that preserved wetlands, estuaries, and other vital natural systems. Around the same time, the Mideast oil crisis sparked a call by Cecil Andrus, Secretary of Interior, to open the entire Mid- and North Atlantic to oil and gas leasing. With the memory of the Santa Barbara oil spill still fresh, this bold maneuver galvanized the environmental community.

I had loved the oceans ever since I spent childhood summers on Cape Cod. My father taught me to fish, and whenever we were on the coast from the Cape to Florida, we would head out to see what we could pull in. Now I saw giant oil companies poised to turn these pristine waters into industrial zones. These waters belonged to all Americans; we held them in common for future generations of fishermen, explorers, and the scientists who might find cancer treatments hidden within underwater corals. Yet energy corporations were ready to put all of that at risk in the name of quick profits and oil addiction.

This was my first encounter with the fossil fuel industry, and I quickly recognized the breadth of its influence. Oil executives had the ear of key lawmakers and the financial resources to lavish on public relations. NRDC, on the other hand, had keen legal expertise and grassroots outrage on our side. In concert with engaged activists and organizations, we succeeded in withdrawing the Atlantic and Pacific oceans from oil and gas leasing—a commitment honored by Republican and Democratic presidents for decades. And yet here we are in 2014 and the oil industry has begun to clamor once again for access to the Atlantic Ocean. It's a sobering reminder that our vigilance must never falter.

I continued to work on protecting ocean waters from offshore drilling, but another threat from the fossil fuel sector was beginning to emerge. Throughout the 1970s, scientists published an increasing number of studies on the "greenhouse gas effect." They had discerned that carbon pollution and other emissions from burning fossil fuels were getting trapped in the atmosphere, increasing temperatures and disrupting climate patterns. At first this realization remained primarily within the scientific community. But in 1980, Gus Speth, one of the co-founders of NRDC, was working at President Carter's Council on Environmental Quality, and he published a report that put the threat of climate change squarely in the spotlight of government leaders.

Now policymakers and environmental groups began grappling with the issue. In 1990, Congress created a national climate research program, and in 1992, President George W. Bush signed the United Nations Framework Convention, a plan to address the climate threat but without firm commitments for reducing pollution. We were thrilled when Al Gore became vice president, as he had already distinguished himself as a voice for environmental protection. Yet although President Clinton gave his first climate speech soon after taking office, he too focused on voluntary efforts to cut greenhouse gases. He signed the Kyoto Protocol of 1997, but it was never ratified by the Senate.

I watched with growing alarm as one leader after another recognized the threat of climate change but did little to combat it. It was quickly becoming clear that climate change was like no other environmental challenge we had seen. In my work on land and ocean conservation, I had fought to preserve one mountain range, one watershed, one coastal area at a time. Climate change affected all places and all natural systems at once. Wild landscapes I had grown to love—from the Adirondack Mountains to the Rwandan forests—could suffer from an increase in drought, storms, and pests brought on by climate change. The ocean waters I worked to protect were becoming more acidic as a result of the pollution that causes climate change, and countless marine species would suffer in these corrosive waters. The health of our families could be endangered by extreme heat and smoggier air fueled by climate change and trigger asthma attacks, respiratory problems, heart attacks, and even premature death.

This was a sweeping peril, and it required a comprehensive response. At first, NRDC deployed our energy staffers in the fight, but it soon became clear that climate change had consequences for all our work, from wildlife to public health, clean water to urban communities. We began to marshal our expertise across the institution. When the Bush administration declared that carbon dioxide was not a pollutant, our clean air experts sued and secured a Supreme Court victory in 2007 confirming it was a threat to human health and well-being and must be regulated under the Clean Air Act. And when the Department of Interior failed to account for how climate change was altering landscapes, our wildlife experts successfully petitioned to put polar bears on the Endangered Species List—the first species to be listed because of the climate threat.

We were proud of our polar bear success, and yet it revealed one of our central challenges: if Americans thought about climate change at all during the Bush years, they associated it with melting ice caps and distant glaciers, not their daily lives. Former Vice President Al Gore helped change that. His 2006 film *Inconvenient Truth*, co-produced by NRDC Trustee Laurie David, vividly portrayed what powerful storms, rising seas, and prolonged drought would mean for our homes, businesses, and cities. The film broke through the clutter and got people talking about climate change in a way no policy or court victory had yet achieved. I had grown accustomed to talking about climate change with scientists and other environmentalists, but thanks in no small part to that film, business leaders, mayors, governors, concerned parents, and people from all walks of life now asked me about it. They wanted to know the scale of the problem, and they started to ask what we could do to address it.

TURNING A CORNER

On a frigid day in January 2009, I joined two million people on the Mall in Washington to witness the inauguration of President Barack Obama. Cheers rose up from the crowd when the president spoke about clean energy from wind and solar power, and a sense of possibility filled the air. Many were eager to put the Bush administration's anti-environmental policies behind us and to move forward with a president who recognized the hazards of climate change and the promise of renewable energy.

President Obama spoke frequently about the climate threat, and his administration helped spur enormous growth in clean energy. And yet, with the economy struggling and two wars to conclude, it took a while for the president to tackle climate change in a comprehensive way. In 2012, his administration brokered an agreement with the auto industry to raise fuel economy standards to 54.5 miles per gallon—on average—by 2025. These standards will save consumers $1.7 trillion at the pump, over time, and reduce oil imports by one-third. They will also cut carbon pollution from new cars in half, per mile driven, the single biggest step the country had then taken to combat climate change.

NRDC spent years working with automakers, unions, and government officials to get everyone on the same page around the need for these clean car standards. Next we turned our sights on power plants—the single largest source of carbon pollution in our nation. The administration has the authority under the Clean Air Act to limit carbon pollution from power plants, but it needed to know it had political and public support. We knew we needed to mobilize the American people to call for climate action.

When I first began working on climate change, experts spoke in terms of computer models and distant projections. Now we just had to look out the window to see what extreme weather was doing to our communities. In the summer of 2012 alone, more than 80 percent of the contiguous United States experienced abnormally dry or drought conditions—the most widespread drought recorded by the U.S. Drought Monitor at that time. Fires roared from Montana to New Mexico, roaring through Fort Collins, Colorado, and destroying 600 homes. At least 50 million Americans were under some form of heat advisory during July, and one freak storm left 23 people dead and 1.4 million without power from Illinois to Virginia.

That same year, Superstorm Sandy hammered communities across the Northeast, including my hometown of New York City. I will never forget the fear and heartache my neighbors and I felt as we watched the storm flood the streets, close down the vital subway system, swamp hospitals and schools, destroy thousands of buildings, and plunge eight million people into darkness across the region.

Climate change has hit home. People around the nation have felt the brunt of this crisis, and they are raising their voices. Americans from all walks of life want to shield future generations from unchecked climate change. And young people are calling on us to turn the tide on the grave consequences our nation has unleashed on their generation.

This is our moment. This is our time to act on climate. We can move our country toward a cleaner, more sustainable future. We have the solutions for reducing carbon pollution from our energy supply. We have political leaders committed to tackling this crisis. And we have millions of Americans calling for climate action.

We now have to make a choice.

We stand, in this country, at a crossroads. Will we power our country into the 21st century by creating the clean energy solutions of tomorrow, or will we anchor our future to the fossil fuels of the past? Our answer will either advance or impede our security, prosperity, and quality of life for generations to come.

TWO

The World As It Is

At its annual shareholders meeting in March 2013, the ExxonMobil Corporation came under pressure from activist investors to begin recognizing, in its business model and strategic plans, our collective obligation to protect future generations from the dangers of climate change. Doing that will require us to reduce the carbon pollution we are pumping into our atmosphere from burning oil, gas, and coal. We must shift, over time, to a lower-carbon economy by reducing our reliance on these fossil fuels.

The largest oil company in the United States, ExxonMobil is in the business of discovering, producing, distributing, and marketing fossil fuels. It is in the business of promoting a high-carbon world. And Chairman Rex Tillerson was unmoved by the voices calling for change.

"What good is it to save the planet," he asked, "if humanity suffers?"

That wasn't exactly the response the activists had in mind. Tillerson, though, summed up brilliantly the central modern threat to our environment. Far too many of us fail to grasp the essential connection between the health of the planet and the welfare of its people, all of us. We often act as if the two were somehow disconnected. That misimpression is deeply imbedded in our politics, our consumption habits, and our economy at large. It obscures the need for change, distorts our calculus of costs to benefits, and discounts the urgency of finding a more sustainable path forward. And it fails to consider how all 7.2 billion people living on the planet can be pro-

vided for without the developed world using an outsized propor-
tion of the Earth's resources. We know we've reached a crisis in our
thinking when an executive at Tillerson's level suggests that there's
some kind of zero-sum contest being waged between the health of
our planet and the welfare of our people.

Nothing could be further from the truth. The great story of human civilization, from its Rift Valley origins to that shareholders
meeting in Dallas, is that all of humanity depends on healthy natural systems for our progress, our prosperity, and our very existence.
Clean water, fresh air, fertile soils, abundant oceans, and diverse
wildlife are not luxury commodities to be considered only after the
earnings reports are in. They are essential to human survival and
well-being. When our natural systems are depleted and degraded,
we suffer the consequences. That's not something that divides us as
pro-industry or pro-environment: it's a basic fact of life that unites
us as people.

What becomes clearer with time is that, across this country and
around the world, resource degradation is affecting people's lives
each and every day. People are suffering from expanding deserts in
Kenya, droughts in Sudan, rising sea levels in Bangladesh, and tur-
bo-charged monsoons in the Philippines. People are suffering from
extended drought and temperature extremes that dry up rivers in
Kansas, bake tomato fields in California, and fuel wildfires across
Colorado. People are suffering from dead zones and oil spills in the
Gulf of Mexico, destruction in the forests of Canada, and contaminated drinking water in West Virginia and Ohio. People are suffering from crude oil explosions on trains in Virginia, pipeline blowouts in Michigan, and toxic chemicals from hydraulic fracturing, or
fracking, operations in Pennsylvania. People are suffering from polluted air, waters, and lands, from unprecedented destruction of
habitat, a global collapse of biodiversity and the widening scourge
of climate change.

People are struggling—not because we're doing too much to
save the planet, but precisely because we're doing too little. Our
voracious appetite for fossil fuels is threatening the very climate
that protects and sustains the natural systems of the planet, our
oceans, freshwater systems, natural landscapes, and atmosphere.
The principal challenge of our time is to embrace and actualize a
clean energy future that veers quickly away from coal, oil, and gas
and toward a more sustainable, efficient, and cleaner energy future.
What will that take?

EIGHT CENTS OF EVERY DOLLAR

It is the purchasing decisions we make, the habits we practice, and the market signals we send that drive the fossil fuel industry across the globe. In the United States, we consume vast amounts of coal, gas, and oil—$1.34 trillion worth in 2013 alone, according to economic data compiled by the U.S. Census Bureau. That's 8 percent of our entire gross domestic product. For every dollar spent in the United States, eight cents, on average, goes to buy oil, gas, and coal.

Here's the breakdown.

Every day, we consume 19 million barrels of oil—about 800 million gallons. That's enough to fill the Empire State Building three times. If that towering edifice were our national gas tank, we'd be pulling over to refuel every eight hours.

About three-fourths of that oil is burned as fuel for our cars, trucks, and aircraft. Most of the rest is used to lubricate our machinery or as feedstock for chemical production and other industrial processes. In 2013, the tab for our national oil addiction came to roughly $2.5 billion—every day. Add another $500 million for natural gas, and we're right at $3 billion a day for gas and oil. And the gas equation is growing.

We're still relying on coal and gas for 67 percent of our electricity, with most of the rest coming from nuclear power and hydroelectric dams. In 2013, the electric utility industry burned 93 percent of the coal consumed in this country and 30 percent of our natural gas. We paid, in 2013, about $1 billion a day for electricity to power our homes, factories, and businesses, with $670 million worth of that power coming from coal and gas.

That brings our national fossil fuel energy bill to $3.67 billion a day, a staggering $1.34 trillion in 2013. And that's how we spend eight cents on every one of our dollars to pay for oil, gas, and coal.

That's more than we spend on national defense—about 4.6 cents on the dollar in 2013. It's more than we spend on Social Security— 4.8 cents on the dollar—to provide retirement income and other benefits to 58 million Americans. It's more than double what we spend—3.6 cents on the dollar—to educate 50 million children in our public schools grades K–12. And certainly it dwarfs what we spend on public oversight to protect our environment. We could fund the U.S. Environmental Protection Agency for an entire year, in fact, for about what we spend every two days on oil, gas, and coal—fossil fuels that took hundreds of millions of years to create and that we dig out of the ground and set on fire.

Our demand for fossil fuels is driving production deeper into our oceans, with mounting risks of the kind of disaster that killed 11 workers and put 170 million gallons of toxic crude oil into the Gulf of Mexico after the Deepwater Horizon blowout in 2010. It is driving production deeper into frontier areas, like the Chukchi Sea and Canada's boreal forest. It is driving production deeper into our own backyards, through fracking operations just beyond the doorsteps of more than 15 million Americans nationwide. And it is exposing communities to the hazards and risks of explosions and spills from the web of pipelines and railroads woven across the country.

Fossil fuel companies make for daunting neighbors. A few years ago, I walked through backyards and driveways in West Virginia towns to hear about what it's like to live next door to mountaintop removal coal mining. I saw homes whose well-tended yards ended on the border of massive strip mines. I strolled with Larry Gibson across land his family had owned for more than two centuries. At one end of his road was a huge mine, on the other side, behind the family cemetery, was another. He was surrounded. Larry and other residents pointed out where schools, houses, entire neighborhoods used to be before mining companies bought them and devoured the land. The amount of demolition involved in mountaintop removal mining is staggering when viewed up close. Those who live near it every day may pay a steep price: a growing body of scientific research has found higher risk for cancer and heart disease in communities with mountaintop removal coal mining.

The threats from coal and other fossil fuels stretch far beyond the strip mines and frack pads and drill sites. The consumption of those fuels is disrupting our climate by choking our atmosphere with dangerous levels of carbon pollution and methane releases from natural gas production. And our continuing and persistent dependence on fossil fuels has empowered that industry to influence, often decisively, the political and economic life of the nation in ways that damage the natural systems we depend on and that threaten our future and impede our ability to seize the manifest benefits of the clean energy economy that is within our grasp.

The impact of this influence ranges far beyond our shores because the major oil companies are global powers. The five biggest players in the U.S. market—Shell, ExxonMobil, BP, Chevron, and Phillips 66—had global revenues in 2013 of $1.7 trillion.

Of the 25 largest companies in the world, ten—Royal Dutch Shell, ExxonMobil, Sinopec, China National Petroleum, BP, Total, Chevron, Phillips 66, Gazprom, and Petrobas—are oil and gas giants. In 2012, their combined revenues totaled $3.1 trillion. If these ten companies were a country, they would have the fifth-largest economy in the world, right after Germany and ahead of France. And that doesn't include some even bigger state-owned behemoths like Russia's Rosneft, Saudi Aramco, or the National Iranian Oil Co. In placing that kind of value on oil and gas as energy sources, and that kind of demand on these companies to produce it, we have empowered the oil and gas industry with enormous financial and political weight. The industry uses that economic muscle to influence, and sometimes determine, geopolitical decisions and the contours of national governance around the world. This equation creates an enormous and powerful obstruction to the change we need, anchoring our future to the dirty fuels of the past and impeding our ability to work together to create the energy solutions of tomorrow. Our job is to change that calculus.

ADDICTED FOR LIFE

Each year, major oil companies like BP, Shell, and ExxonMobil publish their own global energy supply and demand forecasts for the coming decades. These projections are based on a combination of internal analysis by the companies' own staff and predictions made by other groups, including the U.S. Energy Information Administration, the statistical and analytical arm of the Department of Energy, and the International Energy Agency, a 29-nation economic and security consortium that groups the United States, Japan, South Korea, and most of Europe.

In its 2014 forecast, ExxonMobil projected that global oil consumption would rise 24 percent between 2010 and 2040. That would send world oil demand to roughly 110 million barrels a day, requiring about 21 million barrels a day more than oil producers provide today. BP, similarly, projects that the world will be using 19 million more barrels of oil per day in 2035 than it used in 2012.

Over that same period, though, conventional sources of crude oil, those that are comparatively easy to get at and tap, will provide less and less of our fuel, falling by roughly half of today's levels, the International Energy Agency estimates. The difference would be made up by going to ever more challenging environments to assuage our appetite through more fracking, tar sands extractions, and offshore drilling.

"Globally, while conventional crude production will likely decline slightly over the *Outlook* period," ExxonMobil states in its 2014 forecast, "this decline will be more than offset by rising production from supply sources enabled by new technologies—including tight oil, deepwater and oil sands."

Tight oil is an industry term for oil trapped in sandstone, shale, and similar rocks, which can be forced to release the fuel through fracking.

BP cites similar trends in its long-term forecast, warning darkly that "in many cases the extraction of these resources might be more energy intensive, which means operating costs and greenhouse gas emissions from operations may also increase."

BP endorsed investments in energy efficiency, noting that, "It helps with affordability—because less energy is needed. It helps with security—because it reduces dependence on imports. And it helps with sustainability—because it reduces emissions."

But neither company foresees renewable energy making much of a dent in their business. ExxonMobil envisions wind and solar supplying just 4 percent of global energy needs by 2040; BP predicts that renewable power, of all types, will meet just 7 percent of global energy demand by 2035, with oil, gas, and coal each providing about 27 percent of total world energy.

Both companies are counting on oil remaining dominant. Worldwide, oil now accounts for about 95 percent of transportation fuels. By 2040, it will still make up 87 percent of global transportation fuels, under ExxonMobil's projections. We can do much better than that, but we have to face up to the challenge before us.

We all understand that world population is on track to hit nine billion by 2040—a staggering 29 percent increase over just the next 25 years. We know that will mean a dramatic increase in energy demand in rapidly developing countries such as China and India. Unfortunately, much of that demand will be met by burning coal, the dirtiest of the fossil fuels, consumption of which is on track to rise 42 percent in China and India over just the next fifteen years, according to the U.S. Energy Information Administration.

The increasing energy use in these rapidly growing countries is leading the rise in global energy demand and will continue to do so for decades. The United States has the opportunity to lead as well. We must take full responsibility for reducing our reliance on fossil fuels. We must lead in developing and deploying the means of global growth that use energy more wisely than ever before. We must develop the energy efficient technologies that enable us, and the rest of the world, to do more and waste less in every walk of life, from manufacturing and transportation to the way we power our shopping centers, ballparks, and homes. We must take responsibility for our historical role as the single largest source of the cumulative carbon pollution that is choking our atmosphere and disrupting global climate. And we must keep our promises when we pledge assistance to help developing countries cope with the damage and dangers those disruptions are imposing on their people.

Our continuing addiction to cheap and abundant fossil fuels in our cars, homes, and industries and power plants has made it much more difficult for us, as a nation, to put in place and enforce the safeguards we all rely upon for clean and healthy air, rivers, oceans, wildlife, and lands. It has made it harder for us to identify national goals that reflect the mandate of our time, to protect current and future generations from the dangers of climate change. And it has made it harder for us to invest collective resources to achieve those goals by, for instance, building more wind turbines, solar farms, and other sources of renewable power and developing the next generation of energy efficient cars, homes, and workplaces.

This is a problem for the future of the natural systems we depend on. It is a problem for all of us. And the only way to change that is for an ever-increasing number of voices across the country to demand the changes that are required.

Helping to bring about that kind of change has been, for me, the work of a lifetime. Looking back over the past four decades, I'm proud of the progress we've made. But those gains pale in the face of what is required. Our reliance on fossil fuels has developed over more than a century. We won't change that overnight. Transforming our economy, our politics, our very way of life to a lower-carbon model is going to take systemic change. It will be the work not of just one generation, but several. In many ways, we've only begun. Standing together, a nation united around the common goals of safeguarding our children's future, reinvigorating the U.S. economy, and making our country more secure, we must lay out a strong vision of the kind of world we need to create. Then we must unleash the movement that will make it succeed.

THREE

To the Ends of the Earth

On a warm morning in early May 2010, I boarded a small helicopter south of New Orleans and flew out over the muddy delta below to where the Mississippi River empties itself into the green and blue waters of the Gulf of Mexico. Fed by major rivers and lesser tributaries between the Rocky Mountains and the Appalachians, the Mississippi basin drains 40 percent of the United States. On its epic journey southward, the great river ferries minerals, silt, and sediment from the broad middle of the country to nourish Louisiana's fertile coastal wetlands and the waters of the Gulf.

From the time we took off, though, it was clear from overhead that something was terribly wrong.

To begin with, the coastal lands were sliced to ribbons by decades of oil and gas operations, more than 10,000 miles of navigation canals and pipeline routes cut through one of the most productive ecosystems anywhere in the world, triggering mass erosion and contributing to the loss of enough Louisiana wetlands to cover the entire state of Delaware.

Overlaid against that long-unfolding disaster, though, were the marks of impending catastrophe.

The multicolored sheen of crude oil gleamed menacingly atop the surface of Louisiana's estuaries and bayous. A noxious, curdlike film coated beaches and marshland at the water's edge. Flying southeast out over the ocean, I could see rust-colored pockets of petroleum streaming unchecked through open seas. Toxic rivers of crude oil coursed through blue waters and coated large reaches

25

below like some ghastly, impenetrable, poisonous pall. Finally, more than 40 miles out to sea, our chopper tilted right, opening my view to the dark red plumes of oil spreading out from the site of the worst oil spill in our nation's history.

Less than three weeks before, on April 20, 2010, the BP oil company's Macondo well blew out, causing a horrible explosion that killed 11 workers aboard the Deepwater Horizon drilling rig. The rig burned for two days before collapsing into a part of the Gulf called the Mississippi Canyon, in waters nearly a mile deep. As it fell, the weight of the rig twisted apart the steel riser pipe that connected it to the ocean floor, opening an oil and gas gusher from the high-pressure well another two-and-a-half miles below the seabed.

While it was BP's well, two other companies played major roles: the owner of the Deepwater Horizon—Transocean Ltd., a Swiss company; and the Halliburton Company, hired by BP to provide the collar of cement that was poured between the hole that was drilled to reach the oil and the pipe inserted inside the bore hole.

Over the coming weeks, a stunned nation watched in horror as BP struggled and failed to seal the well. By the time it was capped—87 days after the blowout occurred—the well had gushed 170 million gallons of toxic crude oil into the Gulf. That's about 15 times as much oil as the Exxon *Valdez* spilled in Alaska's Prince William Sound when the tanker ran aground in 1989.

Two decades later, the foundation of our clean-up response in the Gulf was virtually the same as we had used after the Exxon *Valdez* disaster—trying to skim the oil out of the water or disperse it with chemicals. The key technological challenge, to cap the well, was one that the industry was unprepared to address. The Gulf—its people, its economy, its marine life, and all it supports—were left to pay the price.

One month before I took that revelatory flight over the Gulf, I had joined several dozen environmental colleagues, members of Congress, business leaders, cabinet members, and others at the White House to hear President Obama mark the 40th anniversary of Earth Day. Denis Hayes was there. As a young graduate student, Hayes helped Sen. Gaylord Nelson, D-WI, organize the first Earth Day in 1970. "And together, they raised their voices and called on every American to take action on behalf of our environment," Obama said, going on to appeal for continued action from all of us to help promote "clean energy that will not only create the jobs of tomorrow, but will also lay the foundation for long-term economic growth." Just hours before, the Deepwater Horizon had collapsed, and those of us gathered to focus on the clean energy solutions of tomorrow were just beginning to learn about the fossil fuel disaster in the Gulf.

What happened down there over the next several months?

About 205 million gallons of oil actually escaped from the well, according to a team of experts led by the U.S. Department of Energy and the U.S. Geological Survey. Of that, 17 percent was captured from the wellhead by special containment equipment—meaning 170 million gallons poured into the ocean. Just 3 percent of the oil was removed from the water, despite months of efforts by more than 50,000 people, many of them working skimmers from a cleanup armada of several hundred boats, according to a second study on what happened to the oil led by the National Oceanic and Atmospheric Administration and the Department of the Interior. When people talk about "cleaning up" oil from the ocean, remember what we're talking about: 3 percent of the oil—almost nothing—was removed. Another 5 percent was burned off the ocean surface, releasing toxic fumes into the air.

About a fourth of the oil was dispersed throughout the water column, either naturally or through the application of toxic chemical dispersants. Another quarter of it either evaporated or dissolved in the ocean, where much of it was broken down by microscopic organisms in the water. And another quarter of it either washed up along at least 1,053 miles of shoreline, oiling beaches, oyster beds, salt marshes, mud flats, and mangroves; fell to the bottom; was buried in sand or sediments; or lingered underwater in the form of tar balls and oily mats that still surface, four years later, after a heavy storm.

The oil killed or sickened untold numbers of marine animals and habitat in a region that supplies 70 percent of the shrimp and oysters produced in the United States, along with hundreds of millions of pounds each year of grouper and other fish species. The spill site itself was home to marlin, swordfish, mako sharks, long bill spearfish, and other species, and plumes of underwater oil the size of Manhattan were documented in waters up to 50 miles from the blowout, creating massive dead zones depleted of oxygen. Coral and other marine species were smothered beneath an oily mix up to two inches thick that carpeted much of the ocean floor as far as 80 miles from the spill site, turning parts of the vital Gulf bottom into what one marine scientist called "a graveyard." And who could ever forget the heartbreaking pictures of brown pelicans—the proud state bird of Louisiana—struggling for life with matted wings in waters fouled by oil?

"It rolls into the estuaries, where everything raises up, your eggs for your crabs, your spat for your oysters, your shrimp," explained Ryan Lambert, who owns Cajun Fishing Adventures, a recreational charter boat business in the lower delta town of Buras, Louisiana. "This stuff is killing from the bottom of the food chain up."

It will be decades before we will know the full ecological impact of this disaster. Comprehensive, long-term research is essential and is under way. Just in the initial months after the spill, though, the U.S. Fish and Wildlife Service identified roughly 7,000 birds, sea turtles, dolphins and whales found dead in areas exposed to the oil. Those, though, were only the tip of the iceberg. For every dolphin that washes ashore dead, for example, scientists estimate perhaps 50 others die and are never found, because sick and dying animals can hide, sink, or become prey to healthier predators. Even these figures don't include the vast array of species in the Gulf, from blue crabs to bluefin tuna, that were exposed to toxic oil that can cause genetic damage, liver disease, skin lesions, cancer, and harm to reproductive and immune systems.

The damage hit hard for tens of thousands of watermen who depend on healthy oceans and coastal areas for the shrimp, fish, crabs, and oysters that provide their livelihood.

"This is what we've been waiting for," Byron Encalade told me on my visit that May, pulling a charcoal-colored oyster the size of his fist from a wire bin, as we drifted through the broad expanse of coastal wetlands in Louisiana's Grand Bayou aboard his 24-foot flat-bottomed boat. "Now it's all about to be destroyed." He tossed the oyster back in the bin and gazed out across the brackish water. "Goin' down the drain."

By then, state and federal authorities had begun closing off vast sections of Gulf Coast fishing grounds, from the mouth of the Mississippi to Florida's Pensacola Bay, out of concern that oil from the BP blowout would contaminate seafood like Byron's oysters. By early June, nearly 90,000 square miles of the Gulf of Mexico—37 percent of U.S.-controlled waters there—were off limits to watermen. The closings sidelined thousands of fishermen and idled hundreds of boats from Texas to Florida, costing watermen hundreds of millions of dollars in lost earnings.

"We don't know how to do anything but shrimp, catch oysters and trap," Maurice Phillips, Byron's friend and fellow waterman, explained to me out on the oyster boat. "That's all we know how to do."

The Macondo disaster basically closed down the three primary industries of the Gulf, the fishing, tourism, and oil industry, for months. People from all over the country cancelled vacation plans along the beaches of Florida, Alabama, and Mississippi. Watermen were idled as fishing grounds were closed. And, despite vociferous lobbying by the oil industry and its congressional allies, the Interior Department suspended deepwater drilling until the facts were known. One spill and tens of thousands of people were put at risk economically across five states.

"THE WORST ENVIRONMENTAL DISASTER AMERICA HAS EVER FACED"

As the ecological and economic damage from the BP blowout widened, President Obama became increasingly engaged. He assembled an emergency task force of cabinet secretaries from the Interior Department, National Oceanic and Atmospheric Administration, the Department of Energy, the Environmental Protection Agency, the Department of Homeland Security, and others, who met daily for the period the oil gushed into the Gulf.

"Already," Obama told the country in an Oval Office address two months after the blowout, "this oil spill is the worst environmental disaster America has ever faced."

In June, Obama created the bipartisan National Commission on the BP Deepwater Horizon Oil Spill and Offshore Drilling, co-chaired by former Florida governor and U.S. Senator Bob Graham, a Democrat, and William K. Reilly, a Republican who served as EPA administrator under President George H. W. Bush. The president appointed five others to the commission, including me. I was honored to serve.

The question before us wasn't whether we should continue to drill for oil in deep water. The question was what went wrong and what could we do now, as a nation, to reduce the risk of anything like this ever happening again. We were asked, in other words, to figure out what lessons we might learn from the BP disaster and apply those lessons to strengthen the public oversight we rely on to protect our workers, waters, and wildlife from the risks of offshore oil and gas production, particularly in deep waters and so-called frontier areas, like the Arctic Ocean.

It was a weighty task. In July, three months after the blowout, we went to New Orleans to hold the first of six public hearings, the rest of which were in Washington, D.C. Over the next several months, we heard from industry experts, regulators, rig workers, watermen, industrial safety experts, and others.

We also traveled along the Gulf Coast to hear firsthand from citizens there. FellowcCommissioner Cherry Murray, dean of the Harvard School of Engineering and Applied Sciences, and I went to Mobile, Alabama, and talked to the port representatives, and then to Gulf Shores where we met with the mayor, local members of the Chamber of Commerce, motel owners, and fishing guides. They told us how hard it had been to rebuild their businesses after Hurricane Katrina ripped through the area, and how they had been working 24/7 to remove the oil washing up on their beaches. I was struck by their incredible resilience and determination facing an uncertain future.

At every public meeting we held in New Orleans, citizens raised again and again their concerns about the health threats from the oil and dispersants. They also expressed their frustration with the total lack of information they were getting about these concerns from the state or federal government. I wanted to reassure them with firm answers, but there was still so much we didn't know about the risks to nearby residents or the men and women laboring for days on end to clean up the spill.

The commissioners, assisted by a dedicated and talented staff led by the indefatigable executive director Richard Lazarus, spent countless hours discussing what we learned, and then, in January 2011, issued our findings and recommendations. What we concluded, in essence, was that the disaster was the result of a long chain of miscalculations, misjudgments, and mistakes, from the design of the well to the drilling operations. Some of the failings were breathtaking; all were both foreseeable and preventable. Neither the industry nor its government regulators, however, prevented them. Instead, multiple warning signs were ignored or missed altogether. Over budget and behind schedule on a job that was costing roughly $1 million a day, workers charged forward in an environment where the operative mantra was, essentially, "Damn the torpedoes, full speed ahead."

While the accident was unique, the conditions that led to it were emblematic of an industry largely accustomed to policing itself, overseen by a regulatory structure that had fallen hopelessly behind the levels of risk presented by what had become a furious race to drill in ever deeper and more hazardous waters. The failures were so widespread, in fact, "that they place in doubt the safety culture of the entire industry," we wrote in our 398-page report.

"Errors and misjudgments by three major oil drilling companies—BP, Halliburton, and Transocean—played key roles in the disaster," we wrote in summary. "Government regulation was ineffective, and failed to keep pace with technology advancements in offshore drilling."

LEARNING THE LESSONS

My time on the commission opened my eyes to the oil industry's drive to operate on its own terms. I had encountered the industry's power in the 1970s and 1980s when I worked to protect the Atlantic Ocean from offshore drilling. In investigating the BP spill and hearing executives, engineers, and officials describe the extraordinary technical prowess they had developed to explore and develop oil resources, I was truly shocked by their massive failure to make an equivalent investment in safety and prevention. I was also struck yet again by the breadth of power this industry exerts across our political and government system. America's hunger for fossil fuels and the oil companies' boundless financial resources give the industry license to function without adequate oversight.

And yet nearly all of the industry's actions—from drilling in public waters and lands to releasing dangerous chemicals—have enormous implications for people's health and safety, with major economic losses to the region as well. Our nation must invest in cleaner ways to power our economy. And the industry must be held accountable.

In the commission's report, we wrote: "Deepwater energy exploration and production, particularly at the frontiers of experience, involve risk for which neither industry nor government has been adequately prepared, but for which they can and must be prepared in the future," In fact, the disaster "undermined public faith in the oil and gas industry, in government regulators, and even in America's ability to respond to crises," we concluded, adding that "no less than an overhauling of both current industry practices and government oversight is now required."

To set industry and government on the path to needed change, we recommended changes in several broad areas:

- a new approach to risk assessment and management;

- a new, independent agency to oversee environmental review and safety;
- more comprehensive environmental review and more robust enforcement of standards that protect workers and the environment;
- more effective spill response and containment capability;
- a revision of the liability rules to better protect victims and provide appropriate incentives for industry.

In a century of offshore drilling, the industry has developed technology and operations so sophisticated it's sometimes compared to the space program. Even the best government oversight can't make that industry safe without an internal culture that puts safety first every time, budget and scheduling pressures or not.

For that reason, we recommended that the industry create an independent institute with a single mandate: to make this industry as safe as it possibly can be.

There was a precedent for what we were looking for in the nuclear power industry. After the partial core meltdown at the Three Mile Island nuclear power plant in Pennsylvania in 1979, the industry created the Institute for Nuclear Power Operations to act as a clearinghouse and standard-setter for industry safety standards. It's been effective at improving safety practices in an inherently dangerous industry, and we've seen similar organizations in other perilous operations like airlines and chemicals production.

The offshore oil and gas industry did take stock after the BP disaster, and it took two important steps, though more needs to be done.

First, it created the Marine Well Containment Corporation, which maintains equipment in the Gulf region designed to contain a high-pressure blowout like the Macondo blast in deep water. What's needed, though, is a fundamental redesign of the blowout preventers to avoid the failure mode suffered by the one that was used at the Macondo well.

Second, the industry created the Center for Offshore Safety, designed to help develop best practices for offshore oil and gas production and exploration. Again, this is an important step forward. Unfortunately, the Center operates under the auspices of the American Petroleum Institute. The API has a long history of developing standards for the industry, but it is also the trade association and lobbying arm for the industry. It is run by the industry and for the industry on behalf of industry executives and shareholders. It is not, in that sense, what is truly needed: an independent entity with a safety mission that isn't compromised by the imperative to make a profit.

When an industry's activities put private lives and natural resources that belong to the nation at risk, there's an essential role for public oversight to play. In the offshore oil and gas industry, the quality of our public oversight had fallen woefully behind the challenge. Our structures were compromised, our safeguards weren't adequate, and the people we depended on to enforce vital protections lacked the tools they needed to do the job.

The agency with primary oversight of the industry was the Minerals Management Service, a bureau of the U.S. Department of Interior. The Minerals Management Service, though, operated under the archaic assumption that it could manage lease sales for offshore drilling and ensure safe operations. In fact, those two responsibilities were in conflict with each other and needed to be separated.

The Obama administration moved quickly to do just that, shutting down the Minerals Management Service and replacing it with two others: the Bureau of Ocean Energy Management, to oversee federal offshore oil and gas leasing; and the Bureau of Safety and Environmental Enforcement, to protect workers, waters, and wildlife.

The commission recommended a number of areas where safeguards needed to be strengthened, and the Bureau of Safety and Environmental Enforcement adopted much of what we sought. In new safety rules implemented in October 2012, the bureau drew on lessons learned from the BP blowout. The new rules required improvements in well design and integrity, for instance, as well as third-party inspections of offshore rigs and production platforms—instead of the former practice, where companies self-inspected their rigs. There were rules put in place to verify the reliability of blowout preventers. Designed to shut down a runaway well, this equipment was in place at Macondo but didn't work.

The Bureau also established a whistle-blower program to enable offshore workers to report hazardous or troubled operations to the U.S. Transportation Department; worker anonymity is protected and proceedings are independent of the Bureau of Safety and Environmental Enforcement. Finally, the bureau chose Texas A&M University to host the new Ocean Energy Safety Institute, which pools industry, academic, and government minds on the use of new technologies, hazardous wells, and training of inspectors. The Institute's

mission is to help coordinate research and to provide technical assistance, education, and recommendations aimed at reducing the
risk of offshore blowouts.

MORE TO BE DONE

Still needed, as of this writing: stronger standards for the design
and operation of blowout preventers; a requirement that companies
conduct formal environmental impact reviews for well sites with
complex geology—such as the Macondo well—or those drilled in
ultra-deepwater; and an enhanced role for science in decisions
about offshore drilling, by, among other things, increasing and for-
malizing the need for consultations with the National Oceanic and
Atmospheric Administration.

The biggest disappointment, for commission members and
Americans overall, has been the failure of Congress to act. For the
U.S. House and Senate, it's as if the worst marine oil blowout in U.S.
history never even happened.

Congress has not passed a single bill to reduce the risks of another disaster of this magnitude happening again. It has not even
endorsed by statute the progress the administration has made,
meaning that those changes could be reversed by a future administration with the stroke of a pen. And it has not raised the absurdly
low $75 million liability limit for spill damages, as we on the com-
mission urged.

Fortunately, BP ignored that ridiculous limit. As of the summer
of 2014, the company had spent or pledged to spend more than $32
billion in clean-up costs, restitution to businesses and environmental restoration projects. The $75 million liability cap, though, puts
waters and other natural resources—in the Gulf or anyplace else—
at the mercy of any company that causes damage it lacks the means
to address. It places the economic risks of company failure on the
backs of the victims and the taxpayers. That's unconscionable. Offshore drilling companies stand to reap substantial economic rewards for their operations. In exchange, they should bear the risks
their operations impose.

Why hasn't Congress acted? The fossil fuel industry, through its
unparalleled influence over our political system, literally owns the
policy. If the industry is opposed to a change—like raising the liability limit or enshrining commonsense safeguards in federal law—

Congress doesn't pass it, regardless of what is in the broader public interest. I saw that up close in my work on the commission.

To my mind, it's a fundamental failing of our democratic system. It's a failing of the people we elect to represent our interests. It's a failing of the voting public—all of us—to stand up, speak out, and demand better. And it's yet one more example, as if any were needed, of why we must reduce our reliance on the dangerous and damaging fossil fuels of the past, invest in efficiency so we can do more with less, and move to the cleaner, safer, renewable power sources of the future. Because to do any less is to ensure that this industry will remain in control of our energy destiny, that our voices will continue to be drowned out in the public arena where it matters most, and that our workers, waters, and wildlife will continue to be placed at needless risk.

In my time serving on the president's independent commission, I learned a lot about the Gulf of Mexico and the people who live along its coast. There's a natural resilience running through this region, and the spirit of its people is strong.

For far too long, though, we have treated this region like some kind of economic sacrifice zone, a place to be damaged, despoiled, and ever further imperiled for the sake of our oil and gas. Setting aside the short-sighted and callous nature of that view, it is simply and irrefutably not true. The Gulf of Mexico, its bountiful waters and fertile shores, its people, its wetlands, its wildlife, are a national treasure. It took nature hundreds of millions of years to create this special place. It's time we started treating it for what it is: a natural gem of incomparable worth, like nowhere else on the face of the planet.

NO MATCH FOR THE ARCTIC OCEAN

Far from the warm and placid waters of the Gulf of Mexico lies another very different body of water, the Arctic Ocean, off Alaska's northern coast. The BP blowout in deep but relatively calm waters was catastrophic. We know how much worse a disaster like that could turn out in the rough and icy Arctic.

That, though, is exactly the kind of debacle the Royal Dutch Shell oil company was courting when it attempted to drill a handful of exploratory wells in August 2012. What happened was surprising but certainly not unexpected. Many had warned that, just as we were unprepared in the Gulf of Mexico when disaster hit, we are even more unprepared for the conditions in the Arctic.

Within hours of arriving at the drill site, the crew had to scramble to move their giant drill ship out of the path of an ice floe 30 miles long that threatened to collide with the rig. An underwater containment rig Shell claimed could bottle up a spill collapsed like a beer can during testing. And, within months, Shell lost control of two drilling rigs, one of which drifted free and had to be rescued from rocks by the U.S. Coast Guard.

The Shell fiasco reminded us that the oil industry is no match for the Arctic Ocean. We have no business drilling for oil in waters where harsh conditions make it nearly impossible to prevent, contain, or clean up the mess from a catastrophic oil spill. And we have no right to roll the dice on the fate of this rich and diverse habitat.

One of the last ocean frontiers on Earth, Arctic waters are home to a rich web of marine and animal life, from the tiniest phytoplankton to the largest bowhead whale. Near the sea live wildlife ranging from eiders and snowy owls to caribou and polar bears. And the Arctic is one of the most productive fisheries in the world, host to pollock, salmon, crabs, and other marine life that account for 40 percent of all the commercial seafood harvested in U.S. waters, the National Oceanic and Atmospheric Administration reports.

Part of what makes these waters so unique also makes them both hostile to industrial operations like oil and gas production and unforgiving of mistakes.

In the Arctic, pack ice makes sea travel all but impossible eight months out of the year for any craft other than icebreakers. Gale force winds can whip up waves as high as a three-story building. By late September the windchill factor makes temperatures feel like 10 degrees below zero. Icebergs threaten ship hulls, propellers and rudders. Maps and charts often omit rocks and other features large enough to ground a ship. Due to its proximity to the North Pole, the Arctic region in general experiences natural magnetic and solar conditions that can disrupt communications and navigation equipment, complicate routine operations, and hamper search-and-rescue efforts. And should an accident occur, habitat and marine life take longer to recover from the damage of leaks, spills, and blowouts than natural systems in warmer waters.

There's one thing more. The Shell drilling site in the Arctic is in remote waters a five-day cruise by cutter from the nearest Coast Guard base in Kodiak, Alaska. Compare that to the site of the BP blowout in the Gulf of Mexico—the global epicenter of the offshore oil industry, home to hundreds of companies and thousands of workers that specialize in drilling wells beneath the sea. It is home, also, to some of the world's most advanced offshore oil and gas production equipment and a vast flotilla of ships, from the commercial fishing and shrimping fleet to the presence of the U.S. Navy and Coast Guard. Still, with all of that support, it took 87 days to plug the BP blowout.

In late June 2013, I stood on the northernmost tip of Barrow Alaska, just at the point where the Beaufort and the Chukchi Seas meet, exactly the area where the industry has focused its sights. Our local guide told us about the Inupiat whaling crew captained by his grandmother. The crews use small sealskin boats, and whenever one of them gets a bowhead, they all work together to pull the whale ashore and share its riches. Even today, the whales provide one of the community's main sources of food for the year. But the crews had not been successful in their hunt for the bowhead that year because the sea ice was still hard up against the shore with no openings to bring the whales within range. Standing on the point and looking out on the endless reaches of windswept ice, I reflected back on the conditions in the Gulf of Mexico where, for more than three months, the industry was not able to contain the BP spill. Does every region of the country have to become a sacrifice zone for energy development? I think not.

"YOU CAN'T FIX IT"

Drilling for oil and gas in the ocean is inherently hazardous work. Drilling is even riskier in Arctic waters, where "cleaning up any oil spill in the Arctic, particularly in ice-covered areas, would present multiple obstacles which together constitute a unique and hard-to-manage risk."

Those aren't my words. That's the assessment of one of the oldest and largest underwriters in the world—Lloyd's, the London-based insurance giant—and Chatham House, a British think tank and policy shop.

Lloyd's and Chatham House assessed the risk of Arctic operations like oil and gas production in an April 2012 report. Their conclusions amounted to a stark warning.

"The environmental consequences of disasters in the Arctic are likely to be worse than in other regions," the report states, citing the difficulty of clean-up and containment in the harsh environment and the comparatively short growing seasons for plants and animals. Those conditions, the report concludes, "limit the resilience of the natural environment, and make environmental recovery harder to achieve." For that reason, the report notes, "Damage to the Arctic environment, if it occurs, is likely to have long-term impacts."

Traditional clean-up methods—which never get more than a tiny fraction of spilled oil out of the ocean under the best of circumstances—are all but useless in the Arctic, Lloyd's and Chatham House found. If more than 11 percent of the affected area's surface is iced in, skimmers, booms, and other mechanical gear can't be deployed without ice-breakers, real-time data on ice floes from ships and satellites, trained observers around the clock, and other so-called ice management measures. For that matter, mechanical clean-up equipment has never been successfully demonstrated in broken ice, where skimmers fail and booms are ripped apart. Along the coast of the Gulf of Mexico, two-foot waves lapped overtop of booms: in the Arctic, where seas run 20–30 feet in fall, forget it. Winds above 21 miles per hour—also common—make it impossible even to burn off oil from the surface. Low visibility, due to persistent fog, can turn out the lights on marine operations of all kinds. And once pack ice sets in, it would be flat out impossible to drill a relief well like the one that finally stopped the BP blowout.

An oil spill in the Arctic, in other words, would pretty much have its way with the waters, marine life, and wildlife—and for a very long time. A quarter century after the tanker Exxon *Valdez* ran aground off the coast of south-central Alaska, dumping 11 million gallons of toxic crude oil into Prince William Sound, oil still lies just inches below underwater and coastal sediments of sand and stone. A pod of orca whales is nearly extinct. And the herring population has yet to recover, putting an end to the commercial fishing career of Alaskan natives like Tom Andersen.

"You can't fix it," Andersen told National Public Radio for a March 2014 report marking the 25th anniversary of the spill. "Once you break that egg, sometimes that's it."

Exposing the Arctic Ocean to that kind of risk is a reckless gamble we can't afford. The Obama administration needs to put on the brakes and put a stop to exploratory drilling in the Arctic. We can't prevent a blowout there anymore than we could avert disaster in the Gulf, where the systems we were promised would prevent or contain a blowout all failed one by one. Nor could cleanup operations save the marine life that died, the coastal areas that were oiled, or the deep-water habitat that was carpeted in crude, despite the best efforts of nearly 50,000 clean-up workers using nearly 7,000 ships and boats in the Gulf. In the Arctic, we don't have the equipment, the knowledge, or the experience to cope with an oil spill if one were to occur.

When the National Commission on the BP Deepwater Horizon Oil Spill and Offshore Drilling reported its findings and recommendations to President Obama and the nation in 2011, we specifically cited the need to address these shortcomings. They haven't been adequately addressed. That's just one of many reasons that Arctic waters need to be put off limits to oil and gas exploration. Any other course would be irresponsible, especially when we have so much to gain by investing instead in efficiency so we can do more with less, and wind, solar, and other renewable sources of cleaner, safer, more sustainable power.

THE TRAGEDY OF THE TAR SANDS

In July 2009, I looked down from a small airplane flying over Canada's boreal forest, a vast and verdant world of evergreen forests, lush bogs of cottongrass, and beaver dams, with crystalline rivers and wetlands that seemed to stretch out forever. One of the last truly wild places on Earth, these woodlands are the domain of caribou that migrate by the hundreds of thousands each spring from the southern reaches of the forest to the northern tundra. Snowshoe hare, lynx, and wolf roam the edges of lakes, ponds, and forested peatlands. Great spotted woodpeckers and ravens make their home year-round in the forest, the summer breeding cradle for millions of North American songbirds like thrushes, flycatchers, and warblers.

But as my plane flew north from Calgary, emerald woods and glistening waters suddenly gave way to an industrial wasteland of apocalyptic scale. For miles off in the distance, as far as I could see, the great forest had been gutted and gouged, a Dantesque nightmare in gun-barrel grey, a dark and dismal vision of the natural world laid to waste. Not a tree was left standing. The land was denuded and carved into a sprawling strip mine. Heavy equipment the size of five-story buildings prowled a maze of roadways and choked the air with dust. And everywhere were open pits of toxic waste gushing from pipelines of steel snaking over the bare ruin of what was once the fertile forest floor.

This is the front end of American fossil fuel demand, part of the price we are paying for our costly addiction to oil. At sites like this and others like it near the boom town of Fort McMurray, the boreal forest is being destroyed acre by acre to squeeze an ultraheavy crude oil called bitumen from underground deposits of tar sands, in one of the most destructive industrial practices ever devised. By the beginning of 2013, tar sands operations had cleared or disturbed about 300 square miles of boreal forest, enough to cover Kansas City. The industry asserts that it is reclaiming mined lands, but the boreal forest cannot be recreated.

Tar sands production means big money for the oil industry. It's big money, too, for provincial and municipal authorities in Alberta, which reckon to pull in $472 billion in royalties and tax revenues from tar sands production over the coming 25 years. That pales in comparison to the value to the industry. The Alberta provincial government estimates there are 168 billion barrels of bitumen available in tar sands underlying the boreal forest across an area the size of North Carolina. At $100 a barrel, that's $16.8 trillion worth of crude.

The rest of us are being asked to bear the costs of that production through the degradation of our environment and health. Communities across Canada and now the United States are experiencing the consequences of tar sands development and being asked to bear the additional risks associated with proposed pipelines, expanded refineries, and future oil spills. Instead of accepting these threats into our towns and cities, we need to create the clean energy solutions that can power our economies into the 21st century.

THREE MILLION GALLONS OF WASTE EVERY DAY

Tar sands are a mixture of sand, clay, water, and bitumen. A viscous, petroleum-based compound about the consistency of tar at room temperature, bitumen hardens when cold—as hard as a hockey puck, the Canadians told me. Bitumen doesn't flow out of the ground—in other words, like conventional crude. Instead, it must be stripped mined, and then processed to squeeze the bitumen from the sand and clay, or heated with steam so it can be made to flow from underground.

To get the tar sands from a strip mine, tons of earth must be carved out first. Once that happens, about two tons of tar sands are hauled out to get one barrel of bitumen.

When the tar sands are buried beneath more than 250 feet of earth—as the vast majority of the tar sands are—strip mining becomes impractical, so producers drill into the ground. To get the bitumen to flow, it must be heated with steam, which is produced using huge amounts of water heated to boiling by burning natural gas. That's right: burning gas to heat water into steam to be injected underground to coax heavy crude oil up to the surface. Some trade-off.

Whether the tar sands are strip mined or drilled into, the process requires enormous amounts of water and produces oceans of waste. After that, the process of separating the bitumen from the tar sands squeezes out about 90 percent of the crude from the sands, leaving behind a mixture of water, silt, sand, clay, and bitumen as waste, or what the industry calls "tailings."

Contaminated by the remaining bitumen—which contains toxic petroleum chemicals, some of which can cause cancer, as well as heavy metals like mercury, arsenic, cadmium, and lead—this waste is deposited into massive open pits called tailings ponds. The sand settles to the bottom, and some of the water is withdrawn and reused in the tar sands process. The finer silts and clays, however, can take years to settle out, forming a thick, wet mud that takes decades to dry. Meanwhile, bitumen floats to the surface as an oily sheen that is toxic to birds and other wildlife.

As of 2010, the Alberta government reported, there were 67 square miles of tailings ponds in the province—enough to cover Washington, D.C., and then some. That figure, though, continues to grow under the pressures of an industry that seeks to triple its tar sand operations in the coming years. Under current plans, in fact, tailings ponds will expand until 2060, Pembina estimates, before the volume levels off and potentially begins to decline.

"In the meantime, toxic wastewater seeps out of tailing lakes at an estimated rate of more than 11 million litres," or 2.9 million gallons every day, Pembina wrote in a January 2013 background paper. "While the public is assured that industry is monitoring and capturing seepage, there is little publicly available information that could substantiate these claims."

Whether by leaking into surface and ground waters that feed the watershed of the iconic Athabasca River or by attracting birds and other wildlife to a poisoned well, these tailings ponds are open wounds on the landscape. They're especially threatening to song-birds and waterfowl, billions of which migrate each year to the United States or pass through it en route to points south.

The boreal forest supports more than 300 species of birds—near-ly half of the species found in the United States and Canada—and

tar sands production is putting millions at risk, the National Wildlife Federation asserted in a June 2014 report it co-authored with the
Natural Resources Council of Maine and several other groups. The
international Migratory Bird Convention protects at least 130 of
these species, including the great blue heron, Canada goose, trum-
peter swan, and the rare whooping crane—the tallest bird in America. Up to three billion warblers, thrushes, sparrows, flycatchers,
hawks, and other birds breed in the boreal forest each year, and as
many as five billion—adults and their young—migrate south each
fall to or through the United States.

"Massive destruction and fragmentation of the boreal forest is
occurring at a staggering pace," the federation reported. "Tens of
millions of birds are ultimately at risk."

"AN ESCALATING CANCER CRISIS"

As horrible as tar sands production is for the forest and wildlife it
supports, there's more. A widening body of scientific research
shows that people who live in communities near tar sands production face substantial health and safety risks that are going largely
unaddressed.

This is a serious concern for First Nations leaders. After we went
to Fort McMurray to see the mining operations, I traveled north to
Fort Chippewa along the shore of Lake Athabasca with Margie Alt,
executive director of Environment America. Fort Chip has been a
way station for travelers since the days the voyageurs began trap-
ping beaver more than a century and a half ago. Today members of
the Cree nations living there are alarmed at the astronomical cancer
rates affecting their tiny community. They told us about their dead
loved ones, even taking us to their family graveyard across the lake
in the delta, and they said the doctors who came to their defense
had been run out of town by the industry and the Alberta government.

Scientists have concluded that the residents have cause for concern. According to a University of Manitoba study released in July
2014, an "escalating cancer crisis" has broken out among native communities downstream of the industrial tar sands extraction operations along the Athabasca River. The study, conducted in conjunc-
tion with the local Mikisew Cree First Nation and the Athabasca
Chipewyan First Nation, found elevated levels of toxic metals like
arsenic, selenium, cadmium, and mercury in the organs and flesh of

moose, duck, caribou, and pickeral, traditional foods that still form an important part of the diet for indigenous people of the region.

"For the first time, we showed that upstream development and environmental decline are affecting cancer occurrence," the report concludes, noting that "cancer occurrence increased significantly with participant employment in the Oil Sands and with the increased consumption of traditional foods and locally caught fish."

Increasingly, the study found, indigenous communities are beginning to shun wild foods that have been tribal staples for centuries in light of government warnings and consumption advisories. All too often, the substitute foods are high in fat, sugar, and salt, leading to a disturbing increase in diabetes, obesity, and related illness.

"This report confirms what we have always suspected about the association between environmental contaminants from oil sands production upstream and cancer and other serious illness in our community," Mikisew Cree Chief Steve Courtoreille told Danielle Droitsch, director of NRDC's Canada Project, when she visited his community in July 2014. "We are greatly alarmed."

SEVENTEEN PERCENT MORE CARBON POLLUTION

The alarm extends well beyond Alberta. The damage from tar sands production is global.

Because producing tar sands consumes so much energy, it also generates millions of tons a year of the dangerous carbon pollution that is driving climate change. It generates substantially more carbon pollution than other types of crude oil that don't have to be stripped mined or steamed out of the ground. That's what makes tar sands oil some of the dirtiest crude on the planet.

If you look just at the production end of it, getting tar sands crude out of the ground in Alberta generates nearly five times as much carbon pollution as the average U.S. crude, the U.S. Department of Energy's National Energy Technology Laboratory has found. What's more, tar sands crude is heavy in sulphur. That means it takes more intensive refining to turn it into useable fuel, and refining is an energy-intensive, carbon-producing operation itself.

That's not, though, where the story ends. The biggest share of the carbon pollution from oil of any kind comes from burning it. So it's important to look at the overall life-cycle carbon footprint for a full comparison.

When you tally up the carbon pollution generated from the time the crude is taken from the ground, refined, and finally consumed as fuel, a barrel of tar sands crude kicks out 17 percent more climate-warming pollution than a barrel of the average crude oil refined in the United States in 2005. That's the conclusion the U.S. State Department reached in a February 2014 analysis.

Why does the State Department care? Because the Canadian fossil fuel infrastructure giant TransCanada Corporation wants to build a pipeline to ship tar sands crude 1,700 miles from Alberta to U.S. refineries along the Gulf of Mexico. A pipeline that crosses our international border requires a determination by the U.S. president that the project is in our national interest. NRDC has done substantial analysis of the issues involved.

NRDC's view, my view, and the view of an engaged public across the country is that the Keystone XL pipeline is not in our national interest, and it should be turned down.

TransCanada's proposed pipeline—called Keystone XL—would cut across the middle of the United States to ship 830,000 barrels a day of tar sands crude oil to a pipeline hub in Steele City, Nebraska, crossing through Montana and South Dakota en route. From there, it would be shipped to Texas refineries in the Gulf Coast cities of Houston and Port Arthur by way of existing pipelines passing through Kansas, Oklahoma, and eastern Texas—right into the "Foreign Trade Zone" in Port Arthur, from which it will be exported abroad.

Put it all together, and the tar sands crude would be passing through states that together host more than 250,000 ranches and farms employing millions of workers and supplying tens of billions of dollars worth of food to Americans every year. It would pass also through a resource dear to those farmers and ranchers: more than 1,400 American waterways, from the Yellowstone River in Montana to Pine Island Bayou in Texas.

That means it would threaten precious irrigation and drinking water with the kind of pollution that contaminated 38 miles of Michigan's Kalamazoo River when a tar sands pipeline blew out there in 2011, or the kind of disaster that dumped more than 200,000 gallons of tar sands crude on the tiny community of Mayflower, Arkansas, when a 65-year-old pipeline blew out there in 2013.

Rare accidents? Hardly. Between 1994 and the middle of 2014, there were 5,758 pipeline blowouts, leaks, or other incidents serious enough to be reported to the U.S. Transportation Department's Pipeline and Hazardous Materials Safety Administration. The blowouts killed 373 people and injured 1,472 more. And they spilled a cumulative 97 million gallons of oil and other hazardous liquids, 58 million gallons of which were never recovered, the pipeline safety administration records show.

What about TransCanada? It's already built two pipelines in this country in recent years. One, the Keystone I pipeline running through the Midwest, had 14 leaks in its first year of operation. The other, the Bison pipeline, exploded in a Wyoming blast that was heard 30 miles away. How much more of that does our country really need?

One thing we don't need—and can't tolerate—is the increased carbon pollution this pipeline would bring. The State Department calculated that the incremental carbon pollution from 830,000 barrels a day of tar sands crude would be the equivalent of putting up to 5.7 million additional cars on the road, about as many as are in the state of Pennsylvania. That's not the total carbon pollution from that oil, mind you: that's just the additional carbon this fuel would generate above and beyond what would be produced by the same amount of average conventional crude. We would have to park every car in Pennsylvania—permanently—just to break even.

Keystone XL proponents claim it would create jobs. Yes, it would, the State Department analysis found: 35 of them, once the two-year construction phase is over. So we're going to ravage the boreal forest, make indigenous people sick, threaten the breadbasket of America with pipeline blowouts and crude oil disaster, send tar sands oil to the Gulf Coast so it can be refined and sent overseas and we'll employ about as many people as your local McDonald's. I'm still waiting to hear how this is in our national interest.

The truth is, it isn't. The Keystone XL pipeline is a dead loser. During his climate address in June 2013, President Obama said he would only approve the tar sands oil pipeline if it did not "significantly exacerbate the problem of carbon pollution." Our analysis shows that the pipeline does not meet the bar the president set.

In the first three months of 2014, we imported, on average, 3.3 million barrels of oil from Canada every day. That's roughly one-third of our total imports, and it's roughly the same as we imported from Saudi Arabia, Venezuela, Iraq, Kuwait, and all the other OPEC countries combined. Tar sand crude accounted for roughly two-thirds of our imports from Canada. We are part of the problem. We're a big part of the problem.

WE DON'T HAVE BETTER FRIENDS

I sometimes hear people tell me that we should support tar sands extraction in Canada because, after all, Americans and Canadians are close allies and trading partners, and our economies and general well-being are intertwined. I've spent most of my life within a day's drive of Canada. My favorite place to be is in the Adirondack Mountains, just south of the long border we share. This is important to me.

On February 7, 2013, former U.S. Senator John Kerry of Massachusetts was sworn in as our Secretary of State—a position first held by Thomas Jefferson. The very next day, Kerry hosted his first foreign guest. It was John Baird—the foreign minister of Canada. Barack Obama's first foreign trip as president in 2009 was to Ottawa to meet with Prime Minister Stephen Harper.

I think that says it all about the importance we Americans attach to our friendship with the Canadians. We share a border 5,000 miles long. More than 300,000 people cross it every day. And Canada is our largest trading partner—more than $600 billion in two-way trade each year. We're neighbors. We're allies, We're friends. But friends need to be able to talk with each other about what matters most. Our future matters—to both countries—and here, we have a problem.

In 2012, we had the hottest year ever recorded in the continental United States. Our cornfields dried up, our pastureland died. It was our worst drought in half a century. We had ranchers liquidating their herds, from the Rocky Mountains to the Ohio River Valley, because they couldn't afford to feed their cattle. Barges were dragging bottom in the Mississippi River. Superstorm Sandy killed more than 130 Americans and did more than $65 billion worth of damage across the northeast.

This is the face of climate change. This is what climate change looks like. This is the toll it's already taking across the United States. We have to do something about it.

Both the United States and Canada have agreed that we must cut our carbon pollution over the coming years. And here's how we're going to do it.

We're going to reduce our reliance on fossil fuels—coal, natural gas, and oil—just like Canada. We're going to increase our use of wind, solar and other renewable sources of power—just like Canada. And we're going to improve our energy efficiency, so that we can all do more with less waste—just like Canada.

Tar sands production doesn't fit with these goals. It takes us backward. That's not in our country's interest or Canada's. That's why it's so important for us to have this conversation with our Canadian neighbors and friends.

The truth is no two countries anywhere in the world are working more closely together to address climate change than Canada and the United States. In fact, no two countries anywhere work more closely on environmental issues more generally than we do.

We cooperate on everything from the health of Yukon River salmon to water quality in the Great Lakes—and we've been doing it for more than a century. We are partners in the Major Economies Forum on Energy and Climate. We are working through the U.S.-Canada Clean Energy Dialogue to create jobs in both countries—scores of thousands of jobs—by helping our economies transition to a low-carbon economy.

That means working to build a smart grid. It means research and development in promising clean energy technologies. It means developing offshore renewable energy. It means the next generation of advanced batteries and other energy storage technology.

That's where the future is. That's where the jobs are. And it doesn't make sense for either of our countries—Canada or the United States—to bet our future on the fossil fuels of the past. We need to power our 21st century economies with the energy sources of the future. And that's exactly what we're working together to do, as partners and as friends.

FOUR

Oil Patch America

On summer afternoons at Theodore Roosevelt National Park, where the Little Missouri River winds its way through the badlands of western North Dakota, visitors gather at the Painted Canyon Outlook to hear a ranger discuss the region's geologic past.

They learn about the colorful sand, silt, and mud that gave the canyon its name. They find out about ancient river channels that glaciers gouged out long before the first humans arrived. They likely hear about the time, some 350 million years ago, when North Dakota looked much like southern Louisiana looks today. It was a place where bald cypress trees grew and alligators roamed a vast swamp that melted away into the broad delta of a great shallow sea that covered the middle of the continent from today's Arctic Ocean to the Gulf of Mexico. And they may also be told how that part of the state's geologic past is tied to the unbridled assault unfolding just beyond the park gates, where, practically overnight, a stampede of oil and gas drilling has turned the majestic landscape into an industrial zone of hard hats, heavy machinery, and razor wire.

Long the open domain of wild horses, mule deer, and bighorn sheep, the gently rolling hills around this spectacular park are now pounded night and day with drilling rigs—one of which greets visitors as the backdrop behind a park entrance sign. Wildlife is forced to dodge the tractor-trailers and tanker trucks that thunder down rural roads and rumble through nearby towns, hauling equipment, dangerous chemicals, and water drawn from the Missouri River. Road signs warn park visitors—some 600,000 a year—of toxic hydrogen sulfide gases leaking from wells along the park's southern rim. Contaminated wastewater is blasted into underground disposal wells. Animal populations are fragmented as drilling operations interrupt or destroy altogether natural migration routes, foodways, and mating grounds. Trucks back up to wetlands and waterways and draw out huge amounts of water used in oil and gas production. Air compressors hiss, pump motors whine, and night skies once lit with stars now pulse with the flames of gases burned off as waste from oil wells around the clock.

"Theodore Roosevelt National Park sits in the middle of a modern-day oil boom," states a 2013 report by the National Parks Conservation Association. "Every element of life is askew out in oil country," said Keith Trego, executive director of the North Dakota Natural Resources Trust. "The roads are destroyed, the countryside is covered with dust, you can't pick up the paper without reading about an oil spill," Trego explained in the summer 2014 edition of the park association's quarterly, *National Parks Magazine*. "It's become a free-for-all industrial zone."

DANGERS BOTH PREDICTABLE AND UNFORESEEN

When I first visited this expansive park in the summer of 1970, there was little to suggest that North Dakota might one day become the second-largest, after Texas, oil-producing state in the country. Driving north from Fargo through fields vast and flat, I had never seen agriculture on that scale, with quarter-mile sections of sugar beets and other commodity crops. We passed by prairie potholes, shallow depressions cut by glaciers that now form some of the best wetland duck habitat in the country. As we cut west toward the badlands, we felt we were headed off the beaten track. That has all changed— dramatically.

The transition began a decade and a half ago, when the energy industry began using in earnest a new technique for tapping into oil and gas trapped in underground formations of shale and other rock. What's relatively new is the ability to drill a deep hole straight down, and then turn the drill bit to cut sideways into the rock. By blasting a mix of water, chemicals, and sand into the shaft, operators can shatter the shale, forcing the release of oil and gas. It's called hydraulic fracturing, or "fracking" for short, and it's changed the face of oil and gas production, not just in North Dakota, but also across much of the nation.

In 1999, there were 58 new oil and gas wells drilled in North Dakota. In 2013, there were 2,176, an increase of nearly fortyfold in the space of just 14 years. By the end of May 2014, there were a total of 7,526 oil and gas wells operating in North Dakota that were drilled for fracking, with another 247 wells scheduled to be fracked in June, the state Department of Mineral Resources reported. The state was producing 1 million barrels of oil and 1.2 billion cubic feet of natural gas, every day, fuels laid down before the dinosaurs roamed the once steamy reaches of what is now an underground vault of shale the size of West Virginia. It's called the Bakken field.

The Bakken is one of six major shale fields where fracking has spiked over the past fifteen years. The others are the Permian field in Texas and the southeast corner of New Mexico; the Eagle Ford shale, also in Texas; the Niobrara in Wyoming and Colorado; the Marcellus in West Virginia, Pennsylvania, Ohio, and southern New York; and Haynesville, in northeast Texas, northwest Louisiana, and a small part of southern Arkansas. There are smaller pockets in California and elsewhere, and fracking is now taking place in about thirty states across the country. Current numbers aren't publicly available on how many wells have been fracked nationally, but we're drilling more than 2,000 of these wells every month, based on published figures for drill rig activity. As of July 2014, fracking operations nationwide were producing, daily, 4.6 million barrels of oil—about a quarter of our national consumption—as well as 40 billion cubic feet of natural gas, 56 percent of U.S. demand, the U.S. Energy Information Administration reports. At prices current as of August 2014, those fuels were worth roughly $700 million a day.

This is oil and gas that, for the most part, we weren't tapping into just a decade before. It's the main reason we produced 30 percent more natural gas and 50 percent more oil domestically in 2014 than in 2004. It's why we've been able to cut our oil imports by 3.9 million barrels a day over the same period, reducing foreign oil to 30 percent of our supply, down from double that level in 2004. And it's why we were less dependent on foreign oil in 2014 than at any other time since 1970—before the first Arab oil embargo.

American administrations, both Democrat and Republican, have long construed oil and gas as strategic resources vital to our economic and national security. Presidents dating back to Richard Nixon have cited oil imports as an Achilles' heel, and have urged the country to reduce its reliance on foreign oil. Over the past decade the U.S. energy picture has changed. The United States has become the world's largest producer of natural gas and the third largest oil producer in the world, after Russia and Saudi Arabia.

Fracking has generated economic growth, but it also has led to greater risks to our health, security, and climate. Natural gas is a fossil fuel, and producing it releases large amounts of methane—one of the most potent greenhouse gases—and burning it puts even more carbon pollutants into our atmosphere. Even as the Obama administration, energy companies, and major manufacturers across the country extol the benefits of the gas boom, the consequences are severe. We must curb the emissions of methane and other dangerous pollutants, protect our families and communities, and implement strong safeguards for production and use of natural gas—and all fossil fuels.

Unfortunately, the rate of domestic oil and gas development has vastly outstripped the development and implementation of needed protections over this past decade. The environmental community has pushed at the state and federal levels to protect people's health, rural communities, special landscapes, national forests, wild lands, important watersheds, and other public places from reckless drilling. And we have done this because fracking entails a lengthening litany of cost, damage, and risk that we've only just begun to recognize. In four decades on the front lines of environmental advocacy, I have never seen another issue that has so alarmed, antagonized, and activated people all over the country.

To begin with, fracking has enormous implications for the water we depend upon. It consumes huge amounts of fresh water, about 2.5 million gallons per well, on average, though in some regions, like the Fayetteville field, it can range as high as 6.5 million. Most of it is drawn from local rivers, wetlands, prairie potholes, lakes, or underground wells, transported on large tanker trucks to the well site, pumped full of fracking chemicals then blasted into the ground, where most of it is taken, ostensibly forever, out of the water cycle. While some of this water—the percentages range widely—resurfaces during fracking operations and a small amount is recycled, more than 98 percent of the total water used winds up injected underground, either as part of the fracking process or, later and after being transported to a disposal well.

Under certain conditions, this toxic water can spill, leak, or blow out of a well. It can spill or leak from trucks and onsite equipment. It can bleed into groundwater supplies, and even make its way into rivers, lakes, and streams, putting wildlife and drinking water at risk, as people have reported in Arkansas, Colorado, North Dakota,

Ohio, Pennsylvania, Texas, West Virginia, Wyoming, and elsewhere across the country. The public seldom knows all the chemicals that are being used in the fracking process. There's no federal requirement that drillers report them. State provisions, where they exist, vary enormously; they are often inadequate and unevenly enforced. One result: emergency responders and medical practitioners often can't get their hands on information about what chemicals a patient might have been exposed to in the event of an accident or spill. One 2012 Pennsylvania law said doctors and nurses must sign confidentiality agreements before oil and gas companies to tell them which chemicals are used in their operations. This left medical professionals confused about what they could tell their patients, but many felt compelled to sign the agreements anyway. Dr. Amy Pare, a plastic surgeon in Avella, Pennsylvania, who has treated local people with unusual skin lesions, told the *Los Angeles Times*, "I just want to make my patients healthy, and I can't do that if I don't know what it is that's making them sick."

Many companies in the industry are providing this information on a voluntary basis through a national chemical disclosure registry called FracFocus. Some states have also decided to require reporting to FracFocus. On its website—fracfocus.org—the public can access information on the types of chemicals and amount of water companies reportedly have used at nearly 78,000 fracking wells nationwide. This is a step in the right direction. But there are also significant problems with the site that limit its usefulness, and reporting of these chemicals is still voluntary in too many states.

I was appointed to a Department of Energy task force to investigate FracFocus and determine whether it is responsive to the public need. As part of the task force, I worked with members of industry, as well as scientists and other experts, to evaluate FracFocus and to develop recommendations for improving it. Despite our widely varying backgrounds, the task force developed a set of unanimous findings and recommendations. The report we produced pointed out that chemicals are all too often withheld from the public under industry claims that these chemicals are proprietary "trade secrets." The report also noted that the data often had errors because mechanisms were not in place to ensure accuracy and that the site unnecessarily restricts access to information. That can make it difficult to evaluate the data on the site or use it to research the environmental and health effects of fracking.

Voluntary guidelines aren't nearly enough. Full disclosure of the chemicals used should be required of companies everywhere and be monitored by professionals with access to the latest health and environmental data, as a part of prudent public oversight. We need quality control mechanisms in place to ensure that the data is accurate. And researchers need to have access to the data necessary for them to study the impact fracking has on our communities. We need to take the FracFocus initiative and make it part of our national mandate to protect the environment and public health.

The U.S. Environmental Protection Agency has identified more than 1,000 chemicals that are variously used in fracking. Many of which are toxic and some can cause cancer. In addition to the chemicals that are added to the water blasted into the shaft, waste water that gushes back up from the well after fracking can contain heavy metals, salts, and other compounds, including toxic chemicals from the oil and gas itself, as well as radium, a radioactive chemical that occurs naturally underground. Improper treatment and disposal of this wastewater has contaminated local water supplies and also caused water quality problems far downstream, as when this waste has found its way into public water treatment plants that lack the capacity to handle it.

Oil and gas production can also release dangerous gases into the air, many of which are toxic or carcinogenic, threatening the health of people who live near the sites. Oil and gas drilling has resulted in dramatic increases in dangerous ozone levels in Colorado, Wyoming, and Utah, and the threat has been identified in other states, including Pennsylvania, Arkansas, and Texas. In some places, researchers have also detected a toxic stew of natural gas-related chemicals, including benzene, a known carcinogen, in the air. Exposure to these chemicals is linked to headaches, asthma symptoms, childhood leukemia, and multiple myeloma.

The wells and associated facilities also often leak methane, a powerful heat-trapping gas that increases global climate change. Heavy diesel trucks that ferry water, chemicals, and equipment to and from the site—requiring many hundreds of tractor trailer roundtrips for every well drilled—can cause toxic air pollution, congestion, dust and noise, and hazard to local drivers.

All of these consequences can imperil public health, rural landscapes, wildlife, and wild lands. Rural communities are becoming industrial centers with heavy truck traffic damaging roads and creating traffic hazards, noise becoming a constant disturbance, industrial lighting turning night to day, and a temporary influx of out-of-town workers putting pressure on law-enforcement officials, shattering the tranquility of otherwise stable towns.

"I DON'T EVER WANT TO COME BACK TO PENNSYLVANIA AGAIN"

In August 2012, I journeyed to western Pennsylvania to visit with people who have experienced fracking firsthand on their farms and in their communities. I met one man who showed me a jug of water from his kitchen sink that looked like rusty mud. Another man's water smelled so awful you couldn't imagine doing your dishes in it, never mind drinking it. And yet another presented a gallon of water from his home, took out a match, and set it on fire—a typical result of natural gas and methane seeping from underground wells into water supplies after drilling. I heard people complain of headaches and illness after breathing air polluted by fracking operations. And I listened as people talked about the loss of a cherished way of life in a place they once loved and had come to fear.

"I can't live here anymore," June Chappel told me through tears. "I have spent too much time crying over this, at what they've done."

In 1988, June and her husband moved to a comfortable four-bedroom home on a 1.3-acre parcel an hour's drive southwest of Pittsburgh. A dream house for the middle-aged couple, it was to be their retirement retreat, a placid sanctuary of grassy lawns and maple trees in the state where June had lived her entire life.

"Now I have an industrial site to look at," she said, explaining that fracking operations on adjacent property had ruined her Pennsylvania get-away and forced her to put her home up for sale. "I can't wait to get out of here," said June. "I don't ever want to come back to Pennsylvania again."

It's no mystery why people like June are fleeing their homes, if they can afford to, in the wake of fracking operations that contaminate their water, pollute their air, turn quiet communities into trucking thoroughfares and put their health at risk.

"The community is not what it once was," another western Pennsylvania resident, Ronald J. Gulla, told me. "The pristineness of it is gone. You don't know what the quality of your air is like. You don't know what the quality of your water is like. There are people here that have all kinds of health issues and symptoms."

Before drilling began next door in 2009, June and her husband signed what is called a "no-drill" or "no surface use" agreement with a production company. The agreement allowed the company to take gas from beneath June's property using wells drilled from an adjacent lot, and to pay her royalties for that gas.

What she didn't reckon on was having an open waste pit the size of a football field two hundred feet from her kitchen door. The pit was used to store contaminated waste water that flowed back to the surface from the well, filled with chemicals, many of them toxic or cancer causing, or tainted with oil and gas from the shale down below.

"It made us so sick," she said, recalling extended bouts of nausea and headaches. "It smelled like gasoline and kerosene."

The waste pit was eventually removed after June complained, but her appeals for the company to buy her out of her property— which she contends is ruined—have fallen on deaf ears. The promised royalty payments, she said, have turned out to be inconsequential. After more than a year on the market, she said in May of 2014 she'd found no buyers interested in living next door to a fracking operation.

PUTTING THE OIL PATCH IN THE AMERICAN BACKYARD

The fracking boom has brought the oil patch into the backyards of millions of Americans like Ronald and June. In some states, wells can be as close as 300 feet to homes. Many states allow drilling less than 1,000 feet from homes. None of these distances has been sufficiently evaluated for safety. And yet, sites are being drilled beneath or near homes, parks, churches, schools, and hospitals. Not even the dead, it seems, are spared, as Don Young learned upon finding that fracking was going on beneath his father's final resting place in the 134-year-old Handley Cemetery in Fort Worth, Texas.

"I would imagine that drilling and fracking and all that vibration is bound to cause some damage," Don told *The New York Times* in July 2012. "But who's going to dig up their dead relatives to see if there's a crack in the casket? What's being done in Fort Worth in general, whether it's to the living or the dead, it's immoral."

In Texas, Ohio, Colorado, and eight other states, more than 15.3 million Americans are living within a mile of a well drilled since the fracking boom began in 2000, an analysis by *The Wall Street Journal* found. That's one in every twenty Americans. And those numbers don't include people in twenty other states where fracking is taking place. "Over the past decade, oil and gas wells have been drilled for hydraulic fracturing in suburban subdivisions, airports, public parks and golf courses," the *Journal* reported in June 2014. While the boom has meant jobs for some and cut oil imports for the country, the paper noted, it also "has left some communities feeling trampled."

Many of these communities are filled with questions. What happens to contaminated water when it sits in the ground for decades on end? Will this toxic fracking fluid find its way into the water table through existing faults below ground? What about the cumulative impacts of fracking operations on our waters, air, wildlife, and lands?

The trouble is residents often feel they have nowhere to turn for answers—or for help when companies run roughshod over their property and towns. Across the nation, state and federal safeguards are too weak and enforcement is grossly inadequate. In Pennsylvania I visited with people who had filled entire notebooks with lists of calls they made to state and industry emergency response lines, with no answers and no response provided. I realized that too often communities have been abandoned by those charged with holding companies accountable and protecting residents from harm.

This has certainly been the case in Pennsylvania, where most of the state sits atop the Marcellus shale. Typical of many places, the state green-lighted widespread fracking before taking stock of its risks.

That headlong rush has had grave consequences for local communities. In just two years—2012 and 2013—there were 897 complaints filed across the state, alleging that oil or natural gas fracking had polluted private water wells or diminished water flow rates from those wells. By the end of 2013, state authorities had confirmed at least 106 cases of well water contamination since 2005, the *Associated Press* reported in January 2014.

Six months later, the *Pittsburg Post-Gazette* reported that fracking operations had damaged water supplies at 209 locations in 77 communities across the western and northern parts of the state during the previous six years, a period during which some 20,000 wells were fracked statewide. The damage included contaminated water or diminished water flows that state authorities confirmed were caused by oil and gas operations. And for each of these complaints there is a family wondering what is happening to its future.

A report by the Pennsylvania Auditor General found that the state's environmental watchdog—the Department of Environmental Protection—was overwhelmed by the impact of fracking. In short, the audit concluded, the authorities were "unprepared to effectively administer laws and regulations to protect the drinking water and unable to efficiently respond to citizen complaints."

That's quite an admission.

A similar story could be told across much of the nation. States, by and large, struggle to find the political will to put needed safeguards in place. Almost universally, they lack the personnel to effectively enforce even those standards that do exist, and they seldom implement penalties substantial enough to act as incentives for compliance. The result: communities are ill-prepared to deal with the fallout from fracking and its consequences, and people are left in the dark when accidents occur.

THE "HALLIBURTON LOOPHOLE"

The industry has been operating for decades without the oversight needed to fully document the risks. And horizontal fracking techniques have only been employed on a wide-scale basis for the past 15 years. We simply don't have much in the way of a track record here from which to draw experiential conclusions. The industry keeps key data to itself. And, absent national reporting requirements in key areas ranging from water consumption to chemical inventories, the industry is getting away with it.

The problem begins with the exemptions the industry secured from so many of our foundational environmental protections nationally. That strips out the tools we need to help safeguard public health and the environment. It precludes the kind of environmental monitoring necessary to fully evaluate the threats being posed by this activity.

This was no accident. I have always viewed these exemptions as being developed with a real purpose by the industry. Before the nation was fully alert to the dangers or fracking or its widespread applications, the oil and gas companies went ahead and carefully secured exemptions to facilitate development. No one believes that the exemptions were secured because there were no issues with fracking, just the opposite.

Before he became vice president of the United States in 2001, Dick Cheney served as chairman and chief executive officer of the Houston-based Halliburton Company. In 2013, Halliburton, one of the largest oilfield services companies in the world, did $29.4 billion worth of business in the United States and about 80 countries around the world. The company is a leader in the fracking industry, with experience in every major shale gas and oil field in the United States. Typically, Halliburton supplies a well owner with the chemicals and sand that go into the fracking fluid, blends the fluid on site with water the well owner provides, then performs the critical operation of blasting, or "injecting," the fluid into the well to break apart the shale deep below.

On January 29, 2001, nine days after he was sworn into office, President George W. Bush established the National Energy Policy Development Group, spooling together selected cabinet-level and other senior administration officials. To chair the group, Bush named Cheney. Over the next three months, Cheney and others met primarily with executives and lobbyists from the oil, gas, coal, nuclear, and electricity industries to hammer out recommendations for a comprehensive energy policy.

The process was so secretive that it triggered a contest between the Congress and the White House over executive authority and the separation of powers. In the end, it wasn't possible for congressional reviewers to determine basic information about who met with Cheney's group, what they discussed, or what impact the discussions had on the group's findings. Cheney's office refused to provide that information, asserting executive privilege.

NRDC filed a request for similar information under the U.S. Freedom of Information Act. Cheney was able to keep the bulk of his records from public view. In an important legal win, though, we were able to review enough task force documents, literally thousands of pages, to establish the heavy hand the industry played in shaping the sweeping energy policy recommendations that grew out of the vice president's work.

Those recommendations became the basis for the Energy Policy Act the Congress approved and Bush signed into law in 2005. The law included a provision sometimes called the "Halliburton loophole," giving fracking a pass on key environmental protections.

The law explicitly excludes the process of blasting fracking fluids into the ground from coverage by the Safe Drinking Water Act. As a result, companies are not required to follow federal well construction rules or reveal to the U.S. Environmental Protection Agency what chemicals they use in their fracking slurry. If we don't know what chemicals these companies are blasting into the ground, it's hard to prove that fracking is the source when contamination shows up in area groundwater and wells, as is happening all over the country. In many cases, without this information, health and environmental authorities don't know what to test for when water contamination is suspected.

The law also created a new exemption for the oil and gas industry from the Clean Water Act and the protections it provides to lakes, rivers, and streams. And it sharply limited the review of fracking operations on public lands and national forests under the provisions of the National Environmental Policy Act, the Magna Carta of environmental law, which guarantees public review and input over projects that require federal funding or permits.

This industry, in other words, doesn't have to play by the same rules as everyone else. Even worse, these loopholes were deliberately created to deny federal agencies and public citizens the basic tools we need to protect our communities and our families from the risks of this industrial practice, which has been booming ever since the exemptions were put in place. That needs to be corrected. This industry needs to play by the same rules we've established for everyone else. Until then, fracking should not be expanded across the country. We need to understand both the immediate and long-term risks and consequences of fracking. Until we do, we need to hit the pause button. That's why NRDC supports moratoria on expanded fracking while we develop answers and advance policies to the welter of concerns surrounding this issue.

The Bureau of Land Management has a special obligation here. It must take the lead by implementing responsible safeguards for the nearly 250 million acres of public lands under its exclusive jurisdiction. This land is a public trust, and the Bureau has an obligation to provide a gold standard of protection to these lands as an example of how we should treat private lands in this country as well.

"A lot of action is needed, and it is needed now," I testified early in 2013 before the U.S. Senate Committee on Energy and Natural Resources at a hearing on natural gas. Jack Gerard, the president of the American Petroleum Institute, and Andrew Liveris, the chairman of Dow Chemical, also spoke. Even as they touted the benefits of the natural gas boom and the hearing focused on exporting gas, I underscored the need to protect our communities, health, and environment. "As of now, we lack such safeguards," I said. "And those protections we do have are no match for the explosive growth in the use of hydraulic fracturing. We have learned, as a country, some hard lessons about the consequences of uncontrolled resource extraction. As we confront the emerging challenges of fracking, we must learn from our history, not blindly repeat it. We must get these protections right. We may not get a second chance."

Meanwhile, local citizens, environmental groups, and some state leaders are trying to fill the gap. In September 2012, NRDC launched our Community Fracking Defense Campaign. Beginning with six states—California, Illinois, New York, North Carolina, Ohio, and Pennsylvania—we're offering legal assistance to local governments that seek to protect their communities from the dangers of fracking. We're helping them to draft local laws and zoning provisions, or to defend existing codes against well-funded industry challenges in court. In practice, this means we're helping local governments assert their fundamental right to protect their citizens when their states and the federal government fail to do so. We helped the citizens of a number of towns in New York state do just that. And we worked with local citizens after the Town Board of Sanford, New York, went so far as to pass a gag rule prohibiting citizens from discussing fracking at Town Board meetings. We challenged that rule on First Amendment grounds and the Board rescinded the rule, a reminder that this is important and meaningful work.

We are also working at the state level to put stronger protections in place.

In New York state, NRDC and other environmental activists have supported a moratorium on fracking until there are real answers to the many outstanding questions about fracking's impact on public health and the environment. Governor Andrew Cuomo has instituted a public health study that may begin to answer those questions or raise additional ones. While we await those answers, fracking is off limits. Other states have considered moratoria as well.

I don't know whether fracking can be done in a way that won't impose huge costs and risks on future generations. Nobody does. We let the fracking horse out of the barn before even asking the question, so how could we possibly know the answer? This much, though, is clear. Our history tells us we can do better. Our future depends on it. We won't get a second chance.

WATER FOR OIL AND GAS

The irrigation canal was dry as a bone. Pastureland that should have been carpeted with a lush spread of pale green buffalo grass two inches high was instead a khaki mat of dust, stubble, and weeds. Wheat fields stretched out barren and parched.

"This is the biggest heartbreaker," Jensen Stulp said, looking out over a parcel of the land his family has worked near Lamar, Colorado, since the railroad replaced the old Santa Fe Trail. "There's not a single wheat kernel in any of that," he said. "We're getting affected by the drought in everything we do."

The summer of 2012 was hard on farmers across the country. It was especially damaging, though, across the Southwest, where water tends to be spoken for by farmers, ranchers, cities, and towns that have a claim on their share of the summer rain before it can even hit the ground. In Lamar, temperatures reached a blistering 111 degrees Fahrenheit three days in a row, shattering the previous record of 107 set half a century before. The record heat was accompanied by something more: the worst drought since Dust Bowl conditions ravaged 100 million acres of the national heartland eight decades before.

And yet, while third-generation ranchers like Stulp watched their wheat fields wither, saw pastureland bake to chalk, and sold off cattle herds they couldn't afford to feed, oil and gas companies consumed enough water in their operations to cover 14,000 acres beneath water a foot deep. That's the figure provided by the deputy state engineer to Golder Associates, of Lakewood, Colorado, for a study the firm conducted for the Western Energy Alliance, a Denver trade association that represents 480 companies engaged in oil and gas development in 25 western states. State environmental advocates contend that the number is conservative and that actual water consumption could be double that.

Either way, as a share of the total water used in the state, fracking operations were small—less, in fact, than 1 percent. Similarly, in a February 2014 report, the North Dakota State Water Commission points out that fracking accounted for 4 percent of the state's water use in 2012, while irrigation took up 56 percent.

But here's the difference: water used for agriculture either evaporates, flows back into rivers and streams, or otherwise stays in the natural water cycle. It isn't buried and taken out of the freshwater system altogether. That, though, is what happens to water used in the fracking process, and the cumulative volumes are huge.

Over the past decade and a half, we've fracked at least 300,000 wells in this country. At an average of 2.5 million gallons of water per well, that comes to 750 billion gallons, enough to cover the states of Delaware and Rhode Island, combined, with nearly a foot of water. Some of these wells, moreover, may be fractured a second or third time in the future to stimulate additional output, a process that can require an additional two million gallons of water, or more, per well.

It isn't as though the oil and gas industry creates this water itself. It comes, instead, from surface water sources—like the Missouri River, a main tributary of the Mississippi; the Upper Colorado River Basin, the lifeline of the Southwest; or the Susquehanna, the mother channel for the Chesapeake Bay—or from underground aquifers that support wells for irrigation and drinking water supplies. Just as important, in many regions when we take water from underground, that causes water levels in rivers and streams to decline, because the underground sources feed the surface waters.

At some point, the question must be asked: whose fresh water is being taken out of the cycle, contaminated, and buried deep underground? Because, in a very real sense, that isn't our water to destroy. It's water that belongs to our children, and our children's children. Who is going to explain to them why it's been poisoned and locked away?

"WE HAVE TO DECIDE . . ."

Just 2.5 percent of the water on Earth is fresh water, and almost all of that is either deep underground or frozen in ice. Even of the Earth's fresh water, just a shade more than 1.2 percent flows through our rivers, lakes, and streams. That fresh surface water is what supports most of the world's land-based animal and plant life, human life included.

The Earth naturally replenishes some of its fresh water, of course, through evaporation over the seas, a portion of which eventually falls as precipitation over land. At the same time, water is precious, fresh water all the more so. Is it really wise and prudent for us to be contaminating scores of billions of gallons each year, taking it out of the water cycle, and locking it away underground forever, without asking the industry that is profiting so richly from this practice to make some provision for ensuring fresh water sources for generations to come? "We have to decide what our most precious commodity is— water or oil?" California state legislator Marc Levine told the Reuters news agency in February 2014, as the state was struggling to cope with its worst drought in centuries. "This is the year to make the case that it's water."

Once water is tapped by the oil and gas industry, it is transported to drill sites, generally by tanker trucks. At 10,000 gallons per load, it requires 250 roundtrips for a tractor-trailer to get 2.5 million gallons of water to a site, where it is mixed with chemicals and blasted into the ground. Some of the fracking fluid stays in the well. Under certain geologic conditions, though, combined with certain well designs, contaminated fracking fluid could find its way into ground water sources through naturally occurring underground cracks and fissures, hydrological studies show. If the surrounding rock is prone to fissures, the fracking process itself can create or widen underground cracks that allow contaminated water to pollute area aquifers, wells, and even surface waters, as attested to by the mounting instances of confirmed contamination.

Some of this water returns to the surface as wastewater containing fracking chemicals and other toxic substances. The vast majority of this wastewater gets pumped deep underground into what are called "injection wells," either for disposal or to force residual oil out of aging wells that have lost their natural pressure, a process called enhanced recovery. There this wastewater is expected to reside—forever.

There is mounting evidence that, under certain geological conditions, fracking operations and injection wells are disturbing the underground structure enough to lead to earthquakes. The U.S. Geological Survey found that the rate of earthquakes greater than 3.0 in magnitude in the central and eastern United States has increased significantly in the past decade. Between 1967 and 2000, there were an average of 21 such quakes per year in those regions. Between 2010 and 2012, though, the total spiked to more than 300. Researchers have theorized that the increase could be related to a concurrent increase in fracking activity. That's all the more troubling given that the region hasn't been seismically active in modern times, so few buildings are designed to withstand earthquakes.

Then there is the matter of handling the toxic wastewater after it comes out of the fracking well but before it is disposed of underground. The wastewater is generally pumped into nearby tanks or containment ponds. Eventually, it is transported by truck or pipe for disposal or treatment. At every step of the process, there's an opportunity for spills.

In 2013 alone, there were at least 7,662 spills, blowouts, leaks, and other accidents reported at onshore oil and gas drilling and production sites in just 15 states, *E&E Publishing* reported in May 2014. That was up more than 17 percent from the year before, even though drilling activity leveled off. As a result, more than 26 million gallons of oil, fracking fluid, fracking wastewater, and other substances were released. That's more than twice as much as was spilled in Alaska's Prince George's Sound when the Exxon *Valdez* oil tanker ran aground in 1989.

Of the waste that spilled in 2013, at least 2.1 million gallons were uncontained, meaning it got dumped onto the ground, into surface water sources and elsewhere, the *E&E* analysis found. The biggest source of the mess: the hotbed of Bakken fracking, North Dakota, where spills spiked 42 percent, while the number of new wells drilled in the state rose by just 11 percent.

"We still have this mentality that we have to go faster and faster," said Don Morrison of the Dakota Resource Council, an environmental group that monitors fracking in the Bakken. "When you're rushing, things go wrong," he told *E&E*.

Those numbers tell just part of the story. Not all states record spill data, and not all track it very well. Some do but don't make the information available to the public. Among those that do keep track, inform the public, and take the extra step of determining and recording the cause of the mishap, the most common reasons for the spills are equipment failure, corrosion, and human error—the very kinds of issues typically dealt with in other industries through the introduction of commonsense safeguards.

Sometime over the long July Fourth weekend of 2014, about one million gallons of toxic wastewater spewed out of a pipe at a fracking well site on the Fort Berthold Indian Reservation. The briny stew of chemical waste ran some two miles downhill to a ravine that leads into Bear Den Bay, an inlet on North Dakota's sprawling Lake Sakakawea that provides drinking water to the three tribes that live on the reservation: the Arikara, Hidatsa, and Mandan. When authorities finally traced the waste several days after the holiday spill, they found it backed up and seeping into the soil, prevented from contaminating the tribal waters by a series of beaver dams.

"We should all be basking in wealth, but we're not," 60-year-old reservation resident Katherine Young Bear told the Associated Press. In her run-down community, boarded-up buildings with cracked window panes share ramshackle lots with abandoned cars and propane tanks rusting in unkempt yards of grass grown wild. "We still have poverty—huge, horrible poverty—on the reservation," she said. Then she paused to consider the oil and gas boom and the damage it had done. "As far as I'm concerned, they should take it away and be done with it," she said. "It's killing our mother earth."

"THERE COULD BE TROUBLE . . ."

Everyone understands there's a lot of oil and gas in shale deposits. But we've put the cart before the horse. As of the middle of 2014, the fracking industry was pumping out roughly $700 million worth of oil and gas—every single day. The resources are there to support the research we need to assess, in a realistic way, the costs and risks this burgeoning industry is imposing on our communities and environment. And the resources are there for us to do everything we possibly can to reduce those costs and risks. To contend otherwise is absurd.

And yet, we are not doing either of those things. Instead, we've actually exempted the industry from standards of conduct we require of others. That doesn't make sense. In fact, it's unconscionable.

We should be reducing our reliance on oil and gas instead of forging ahead and recklessly squeezing from our lands every drop or cubic foot we can find. Meanwhile, if the shale boom is so important, why wouldn't we take the time and invest the resources required to reduce needless cost and risk to our communities? Isn't that the best way to ensure the long-term viability of a valued industry?

George Mitchell certainly thought so. The pioneering Texas oilman widely regarded as the father of modern fracking, Mitchell spoke with *Forbes* in July 2012, a year and a half before he died.

"The administration is trying to tighten up controls. I think it's a good idea," Mitchell told the magazine. "They should have very strict controls."

Mitchell, who died in December 2013 at the age of 94, understood better than most the risks of reckless fracking. He didn't trust industry wildcatters to always do the right thing. He worried about the damage that irresponsible industry actors might do. And he thought meeting safety and environmental standards was a reasonable cost of doing business that should be reflected in the price of gas. How do you argue against that and still claim to support the free market?

Why, though, was public oversight necessary, Mitchell was asked in the interview.

"Because if they don't do it right," Mitchell said, referring to fracking company operations, "there could be trouble."

One month later, Mitchell laid out exactly the kinds of safeguards he thought the industry needs, in an op-ed he wrote jointly with Michael Bloomberg, who was the mayor of New York City at the time.

"The rapid expansion of fracking has invited legitimate concerns about its impact on water, air and climate—concerns that the industry has attempted to gloss over," Mitchell and Bloomberg wrote, in an August 2012 op-ed published in *The Washington Post.* "With so much at stake for the environment, jobs and energy security," the men wrote, "it is critical that we make reasoned decisions about how to manage the use of hydraulic fracturing technology."

They called for standards that would:

- require companies to disclose all chemicals used in the fracking process;
- set requirements for the design, construction, and operation of wells;
- minimize water consumption, protect groundwater, and ensure proper disposal of fracking wastewater;
- improve controls on air pollution and require leaking methane to be captured;
- reduce the industry's impact on roads, ecosystems, and communities.

These measures would go a long way toward reducing the costs and risks that right now this industry is imposing on the natural systems we depend on, our people and the communities where we live.

But we need to do more.

We have to begin by holding oil and gas companies to account for the costs, damage, and risks of fracking. The first step is to close the "Halliburton loophole" and end the industry's exemptions from key provisions of bedrock environmental protections like our Clean Water Act, Clean Air Act, Safe Drinking Water Act, National Environmental Policy Act, and hazardous waste rules. This industry needs to be held to the same standards as others that engage in activities that have the potential to do widespread and lasting harm to our environment and our health. Standards for well siting, design, and construction have to be as strong as possible. We have to keep fracking off of our nation's last wild places, like our national forests, and away from schools, residential areas, and large municipal drinking water supplies. We must red-zone these areas and place them completely off limits to fracking. And we need to ensure that communities everywhere are allowed to protect themselves, safeguard their future, and reflect the values of their residents by restricting or banning fracking within their borders, including through comprehensive zoning laws and planning provisions.

Once again, though, I'm going to be absolutely candid. Even if we were to put all these protections in place, it is not at all clear that fracking can be done in a way that is sustainable and safe. There are just too many unanswered questions about the risks to public health, our environment, and even our climate.

That's why we at NRDC have supported proposed moratoria in states around the country. Quite clearly, if we don't have the answers, we shouldn't be subjecting communities to industry experimentation.

When it comes to the fossil fuel industry, we've been here before.

"The lessons provided by the history of science and technology concerning all major energy sources and many other industrial initiatives show that substantial environmental impacts were typically not anticipated. What is perhaps more alarming is that where substantial adverse impacts were anticipated, these concerns were dismissed or ignored by those who embraced the expected positive benefits of the economic activities that produced those impacts," the Council of Canadian Academies wrote in a 2014 report on fracking it prepared for the federal Minister of Environment, roughly Canada's equivalent of the U.S. Environmental Protection Agency. "Whether or not shale gas development will turn out in the long term to have been a positive or negative influence on global well-being will depend on how society understands this technology and manages it."

In other words, we're rolling the dice, to a very large extent, when it comes to the risks of fracking. We don't know what we're dealing with, we haven't done what's required to find out, and we haven't taken the basic precautions that any sound risk-management analysis would dictate as prudent. That's not good enough—not in North Dakota, not in Pennsylvania, not in anywhere in the United States. We can do a lot better than that—and we must.

"IT SOUNDED LIKE A SUPER-SIZE DEEP FRYER"

Just after lunchtime on the last day of April 2014, a train more than a mile long rumbled into the central Virginia town of Lynchburg in the foothills of the Blue Ridge Mountains. Since the nation's beginnings, Appalachian coal has passed through the town, first by boat down the James River to the factories of Richmond and the ports at

Hampton Roads, and later on the railroad built alongside the river. This train, though, was carrying something different, about three million gallons of crude oil from the Bakken fields of North Dakota and Montana, bound for a terminal near the Chesapeake Bay and from there by barge to East Coast refineries.

While rounding a gentle curve, thirteen cars jumped the track. Three ruptured and ignited, sending a horrifying fireball rocketing skyward, before sliding down the bank, spreading a carpet of flame across the river's surface and dumping 29,000 gallons of crude oil into the water.

"It sounded like a super-size deep fryer just going at it," Mason Basten told *The News & Advance* of Lynchburg, after watching the train wreck from his boat shop on the opposite shore. "I think we have a big damn mess, and hopefully this won't be an environmental disaster."

The river was running high, near flood stage. Black oil coated vegetation along the river's edge for nearly a half mile downstream. By late the next day an oily sheen glistened on the surface of water passing through Richmond, some 140 miles downstream. "As the floodwaters recede, oil deposits are being seen on the banks of the river and vegetation that had been underwater," the James River Association, a non-profit group, noted in a statement. River bottom sediment samples taken a month after the spill found oil and toxic chemicals from the spill in the river bottom, the group found, posing a potential threat to spawning shad and herring.

It's more than 1,400 miles from Virginia to the Bakken oil fields, but that hasn't spared the Old Dominion from the risks of the fracking boom. Since the end of 2013, up to five oil trains have passed through the state each week, with each one typically carrying some three million gallons of Bakken crude through a stretch that spans 20 counties.

Far from an exception, Virginia mirrors a national trend. Bakken oil production in North Dakota has far outstripped the capacity of pipeline companies to move it to refineries. Instead, close to 25 million gallons of Bakken crude—roughly 60 percent of North Dakota's production—is shipped out every day on long trains of tank cars. That's why crude oil shipments by rail jumped more than 4,000 percent between 2008 and 2013, bringing the threat of explosions, fire, and widespread pollution to thousands of communities large and small, whose residents never imagined such risks would touch their lives.

"It's difficult to get Virginia to pay attention to this because they don't think of their being part of the oil patch, but now they are," Fred Millar, a Virginia hazardous materials safety consultant, told the *Richmond Times-Dispatch* on the day of the Lynchburg accident. "Virginia is being used as a transportation corridor only," he said. "We get all of the risks and no benefits."

In 2008, the nation's railroads delivered 9,500 carloads of crude oil nationwide, the Association of American Railroads, an industry trade group, reported in a June 2014 study called *Moving Crude Oil by Rail*. By 2013, that number had surged to nearly 408,000 carloads. That's an increase of more than fortyfold, in just five years.

In 2008, railroads delivered a total of 6.7 million barrels of oil, about as much as we consume in this country every nine hours. By the summer of 2014, railroads were on track to move 450 million barrels of crude oil for the year, as much as the country consumes every 24 days.

One week after the Lynchburg derailment cast a spotlight on the issue, the U.S. Department of Transportation weighed in, declaring that the "startling" surge in Bakken crude oil rail accidents was proof that such shipments pose "an imminent hazard" to the nation. Crude oil shipments by rail, the DOT concluded, are "presenting a substantial likelihood that death, serious illness, severe personal injury, or a substantial endangerment to health, property, or the environment may occur."

A NATIONAL RISK

In 2013, U.S. railroads spilled more crude oil—1.2 million gallons—than they did in the previous four decades combined, McClatchy Newspapers reported. The analysis relied on data provided by the U.S. Pipeline and Hazardous Materials Safety Administration, an oversight bureau of the U.S. Transportation Department.

The basic problem is that neither our railroad system, nor, for the most part, the tank cars being used to haul this crude were designed to carry highly combustible liquids. The rail system's not up to the task, and it's being used anyway, chiefly to carry crude oil from the Bakken fields of North Dakota. By April 2014, those fields were producing an average of 42 million gallons of crude oil every day, a twelvefold increase from just a decade before. With only 34 percent of that being shipped out by pipeline, as of spring of 2014, the rest moves out on trains like the one that blew up in Lynchburg.

Ordinary crude oil doesn't necessarily explode in a crash. But Bakken crude—like oil from other shale deposits in parts of Texas, Colorado, Wyoming, and elsewhere—contains high levels of flammable gases, compared with more conventional crudes. That means this kind of crude has a greater propensity to ignite in crashes.

Industry recognizes the problem. In South Texas, for example, energy companies invested hundreds of millions of dollars in equipment called stabilizers, which remove the most volatile gases from the crude before it is shipped, making it more stable and less prone to explosion. Only one such unit was being readied for the Bakken fields, *The Wall Street Journal* reported in July 2014, noting that, privately, some pipeline companies refused to transport Bakken crude that hadn't first been stabilized, out of fear it would cause a pipeline explosion.

"In North Dakota's Bakken Shale oil field, nobody installed the necessary equipment," the *Journal* reported in a July 7 article. As a result, the report continued, the Bakken "is producing oil that pipelines often would reject as too dangerous to transport."

And so it winds up on trains instead, exposing people and communities along the rail lines that ferry this dangerous freight to the growing risk of death, injury, and environmental contamination. Indeed, North Dakota is counting on rail carrying more and more Bakken crude to market.

"Crude oil take away capacity is expected to remain adequate as long as rail deliveries to coastal refineries keep growing," the North Dakota Department of Mineral Resources stated in a July 2014 update of oil and gas production figures.

As railroads ferry more and more crude oil, the risks of transporting potentially explosive cargo touches a growing number of communities nationwide. ForestEthics, a San Francisco environmental group, estimates that 25 million Americans live within a mile of a rail line that regularly carries crude oil. The group based its estimate on a conservative reading of industry data and posted its findings, with a map of the rail routes, on a website named "Oil Train Blast Zone." It shows a web of oil train routes crisscrossing the country, from Philadelphia to Los Angeles; from the rail hubs of Chicago, Kansas City, and Memphis to the refinery centers of Houston, New Orleans, and Long Beach and every crossroads and way station in between.

There's a route that ferries this combustible cargo the entire length of New York state, from the Canadian border to the New Jersey suburbs of New York City, passing through the Champlain

Valley, along 60-plus miles of lake shore with the Green Mountains on one side and the Adirondacks on the other. This is rural America, where volunteer fire departments struggle to maintain the equipment they need to put out a house fire.

Most municipal and local fire departments had no idea these combustible shipments were passing through their communities until the spring of 2014, when federal authorities began to require a heads up in the wake of the Lynchburg derailment. Even so, not even the fire departments of major cities have the special training, equipment, and supplies of chemical foam needed to combat the forces of oil by the tanker car bursting into flames.

"If one of them wrecks, state and local emergency responders don't have the equipment needed to put out a catastrophic fire," the Minneapolis *Star Tribune* reported in February 2014. Eight oil trains a mile-long each roll through Minnesota every day, on average, and six of those pass through Minneapolis and St. Paul. "We are ill-prepared for this," state Representative Frank Hornstein of the Democratic-Farmer-Labor party told the paper. "This is overwhelming the state right now."

And if the Twin Cities don't have what it takes to tame an oil train fire, imagine the situation for tiny Americus, Georgia, one of thousands of rural communities these trains pass through.

The risks of this widening game of Russian roulette came tragically to light in July 2013, when an unattended runaway train hauling 72 tank cars loaded with Bakken crude derailed on a curve and exploded into flames, killing 47 people and destroying the historic center of the Canadian town of Lac-Megantic in the province of Quebec. The train spilled some 1.5 million gallons of oil, an unknown amount of which poured into the Chaudiere River. Oil was still in the water a month later, and environmental clean-up costs were estimated at $7.7 million.

Four months after that, nearly 750,000 gallons of Bakken crude spilled and caught fire when a train derailed in rural wetlands outside of Aliceville, Alabama. The next month, December 2013, trains collided in Casselton, North Dakota, bursting into flames and releasing more than 400,000 gallons of Bakken crude. Many of the town's 2,400 residents were forced to evacuate their homes in subzero temperatures.

"OUR SAFETY REGULATIONS NEED TO CATCH UP"

On January 23, 2014, the National Transportation Safety Board (NTSB), an independent federal agency charged with investigating transportation accidents, joined with its Canadian counterpart, the Transportation Safety Board of Canada, to call for strengthened safeguards to address the growing risks of shipping crude oil by rail.

"The NTSB is concerned that major loss of life, property damage and environmental consequences can occur when large volumes of crude oil or other flammable liquids are transported on a single train involved in an accident, as seen in the Lac-Megantic, Quebec, accident, as well as several accidents the NTSB has investigated in the U.S.," the Safety Bureau said in a prepared statement.

"The large-scale shipment of crude oil by rail simply didn't exist ten years ago, and our safety regulations need to catch up with this new reality," said NTSB chairman Deborah A. P. Hersman. "While this energy boom is good for business, the people and environment along rail corridors must be protected from harm."

There are three key problems: where this hazardous oil is going, the level of public oversight it receives en route, and what it's traveling in. The NTSB has suggested improvements in all three areas, but it hasn't gone far enough.

The NTSB and its Canadian partner recommended that railroads review their routing options with an eye toward reducing the exposure of major urban areas to the risks of crude oil shipping. That's a good first step, but we need to direct trains hauling explosive crude oil to steer clear of population centers, period.

The NTSB said railroad companies should be audited regularly to ensure that oil trains have the ability to respond to a catastrophic accident and loss of oil. Again, yes, but the suggestion rings hollow without the personnel to implement it and local support to make it more effective. The Federal Railroad Administration—the rail safety arm of the U.S. Department of Transportation—employs 400 inspectors nationwide. Working with about 170 state safety inspectors, these officials oversee the handling of hazardous materials like crude oil, track conditions, passenger rail service, operating practices, and a dozen other key areas for operations stretched out over many thousands of miles of rail. This inspection force needs to be increased to reflect the growing risks of crude oil shipments. Local governments should keep crude oil terminals at least a mile away from homes, schools, hospitals, day care centers, churches, and other sensitive sites. And states should levy fees on crude oil shippers and carriers to help pay for the emergency response services necessary to protect the public from the risks these trains impose.

Finally, we need to stop transporting crude oil in tank cars that were never intended to ship explosive liquids and are not up to the task. The NTSB has warned us for decades that these tank cars, built to a federal standard designated DOT-111, are no match for the dangers of shipping flammable liquids like the Bakken crude. Within the railroad industry and among safety experts, these cars are variously derided as "soda cans," "rolling bomb shells" or even "the Ford Pinto of rail cars." A 1991 NTSB investigation found that the DOT-111 tank cars burst open in crashes more than twice as often as those build to more rigorous standards of safety and strength. The NTSB administrator at the time, Gilbert Carmichael, wrote in a formal safety recommendation that he was "extremely concerned" about the risks this class of tank car posed to human life, property, and the environment when used to ship flammable fuels and other types of hazardous liquids.

More than two decades later by the industry's own reckoning, these cars account for two-thirds of the 335,000 tank cars in the nation's fleet. As of mid-2014, nearly 100,000 of these risky tank cars were hauling dangerous Bakken crude or other flammable liquids through communities across the country.

In July 2014 the Pipeline and Hazardous Safety Administration proposed banning the use of these cars to haul explosive crude oil, with the unsafe tankers to be phased out of use over the next two years. In addition, the agency proposed new speed limits, restricting DOT-111 tankers to a maximum speed of 40 miles per hour when they are carrying flammable materials. Final implementation of the rules was awaiting comment from industry and other stakeholders as of the fall of 2014.

Meanwhile, why are we allowing these cars, these "soda cans," to transport millions of gallons of dangerous crude oil by rail through our cities, towns, and communities—every single day—putting billions of dollars worth of property, priceless natural resources, and the lives of some 25 million of our people in harm's way? We should stop hauling Bakken crude oil in these unsafe tank cars immediately.

It isn't that the railroad industry hasn't acted—requiring modifications to help make existing and future tank cars stronger and more resistant to rupture, looking for ways to reduce the amount of oil snaking its way by rail through population centers, and volunteering to honor a 40-mile-per-hour speed limit for trains hauling crude oil in the older tank cars through 46 major urban areas. The industry, though, hasn't done nearly enough to address the full range of safety risks and environmental challenges associated with the spike in crude oil deliveries.

We'll never make it completely safe to ship Bakken crude oil by rail. But we must do everything possible to reduce the risk as much as we can. That begins by ending the use of tank cars that were never meant to carry explosive crude oil. And, beyond that, we must take a systemic approach to safeguards that include speed restrictions, route modifications, inspections, and proper identification of the hazards of shipping this crude oil. That's the minimum we must do to ensure that we're doing all we can to prevent the kinds of tragic accidents that have become far too common throughout our country.

A FALSE CHOICE

Of course, proponents of the Keystone XL tar sands pipeline point to rail safety issues as a reason to green light the misguided scheme to pipe some of the dirtiest fuel on the planet through the American breadbasket so it can be refined on our Gulf Coast and shipped overseas. We haven't been presented, in this country, with a choice between pipeline or rail. The industry wants both, is using both, and is planning to expand both.

The Keystone XL is a bad idea. It needs to be denied. We would be far better off investing that money in infrastructure that supports the clean energy solutions of the future, instead of doubling down to perpetuate our reliance on the dangerous fossil fuels of the past. And, however we transport crude oil, we need to recognize the dangers and put in place commonsense safeguards so we don't continue to put the lives of our people, the fate of our communities, and the health of our environment at needless and preventable risk. Surely we can all agree on that.

The oil and rail industries know how to do this, but their investment in safety has paled in comparison to the skyrocketing delivery of oil by rail. A year after the Lac-Megantic disaster, industry had implemented only half steps—at best—to reduce the hazards of shipping crude oil by rail. The fossil fuel industry and those that support it are constantly assailing public oversight. They resist federal safeguards as a matter of course. And yet, in the face of a clear and growing public danger, the response from the private sector has been anemic.

Once again we see that when the profit motive undercuts the necessity of protecting our people and resources, action by the fossil fuel industry cannot be counted on as a substitute for effective public oversight. That is exactly why national safeguards are so important.

Meanwhile, it is Americans in places like Aliceville, Casselton, Lynchburg, and countless other communities across this country that are bearing the risk and paying the price of additional oil train disasters. That's one more part of the price we're paying for our persistent addiction to fossil fuels. And it's one more reason we need to get serious about reducing our reliance on these dirty, dangerous, and destructive fuels.

FIVE

A Widening Scourge

A fifth-generation Iowa farmer, Matt Russell is used to trudging out in the snow after dark to make sure his cattle have hay for the night. This time, though, something seemed strange. Russell turned his face against the blizzard that would drop a foot of snow on his farm that night, and then he heard the sound of the frogs in the pond. It was the third night of May in 2013.

"I suppose there are some places in the world where there are frogs in the snow, but not in Iowa," Russell told a group of U.S. House of Representatives members at a climate change forum a few months later. "This is one of the things that climate change means— the wrong weather at the wrong time."

After decades of stark warnings about widening deserts, melting ice and rising sea levels, the impacts of global climate change have hit home for Americans nationwide. Where once we looked to gloomy projections for a foretaste of the dangers to come, now all we have to do is look out the window. From our cities and communities to our ranches and farms, in our forests, fields, mountains, and streams, the signs of climate chaos are everywhere.

California spent 2014 in the grip of its worst drought since at least the late 1800s, when recordkeeping began. Traveling there throughout the year, I was alarmed flying over the Sierra Nevada mountains and looking down on snowpack—one of three sources of the state's water—at just 18 percent of its normal level. Underground aquifers that supply 65 percent of California's water were being rapidly depleted, and water levels were dropping along the state's third main source, the Colorado River Basin. By early September, more than 80 percent of the state was experiencing severe drought. Fish died in algae sludge in the shallows of vanishing waterways, river bottoms were reduced to dry stones and puddles, and boats lay marooned like corpses atop the cracked beds of dried lakes. I heard firsthand the concerns of people who saw farm fields left to lie fallow, rural towns laying in stocks of bottled water and residents around the state bracing for an extended wildfire season. Droughts have hit California before, but climate change is making them more frequent and severe. Chances are growing for what scientists call a southwestern "megadrought" lasting a decade or more, according to a study by researchers from the University of Arizona, Cornell University, and the U.S. Geological Survey. "As we add greenhouse gases into the atmosphere—and we haven't put the brakes on stopping this—we are weighting the dice for megadrought," explained Toby Ault, assistant professor of earth and atmospheric sciences and lead author of a September 2014 paper on the research.

We see the signs of equally uncertain futures across the nation. Ohio corn fields barren and parched from epic drought. Streets routinely swamped whenever the moon is full over Miami, Charleston, and Norfolk due to rising sea level. Colorado wildfires raging uncontrolled as heat dries out forests thirsting for rain. Kansas cattle with no pasture to graze. Crippling heat waves in Dallas, Detroit, and Washington D.C. Water levels falling in aquifers across the Great Plains. Maple syrup makers wanting for sap in Vermont. High-elevation pine forests dying in Yellowstone National Park. As I write this from the Adirondack Mountains, invasive species like the hemlock woolly adelgid and the emerald ash borer are moving into the surrounding forest, changing forever an iconic wilderness that has attracted Americans for more than a century. Not even our proudest urban centers are beyond the reach of climate chaos, as those of us who live in New York City learned in October 2012 when Hurricane Sandy killed 159 people across the region, left 23,000 homeless, put 14 feet of water on the streets of lower Manhattan, and shut down the New York Stock Exchange for two days. It was devastating to see this destructive power unleashed in my hometown.

These consequences, and more, are just a sampling of the price we already are paying in our daily lives for global climate change happening now. Those costs, moreover, merely hint at the even greater risks we face and the mounting damage to come unless we act now to reduce the dangerous carbon pollution from burning fossil fuels that is driving climate chaos.

"There is a time for weighing evidence and a time for acting," former U.S. Treasury Secretary Henry Paulson wrote June 22, 2014, in *The New York Times*. "We're staring down a climate bubble that poses enormous risks to both our environment and our economy.The warning signs are clear and growing more urgent as the risks go unchecked. . . . We need to act now."

WE KNOW WHAT'S HAPPENING TO OUR CLIMATE

Every single authoritative source on the subject has been warning us for years with evidence that grows more compelling and in language that becomes more urgent with each passing year. Now events are overrunning the warnings. Climate change is no longer some vague and theoretical threat of the future. It's a global crisis with backyard footprints. It is now touching all of us, wherever we live.

"Climate change, once considered an issue for a distant future, has moved firmly into the present," the U.S. National Climate Assessment reported in May 2014 in the most authoritative and comprehensive study ever conducted on the actual impact climate change is having on our country. "Americans are noticing changes all around them," the assessment concludes. "While scientists continue to refine projections for the future, observations unequivocally show that climate is changing and that the warming of the past 50 years is primarily due to human-induced emissions of heat-trapping gases. These emissions come mainly from burning coal, oil, and gas, with additional contributions from forest clearing and some agricultural practices."

Those are the findings of the U.S. Global Change Research Program. It was established in 1989 by President George H. W. Bush and mandated by the U.S. Congress the next year to develop the rock-bottom indisputable truth about climate change, so that our policymakers would have the facts they need to make informed decisions about what is in the best interest of our country going forward.

The program pulls together the expertise of thirteen federal agencies, from the National Science Foundation and the Department of Commerce to the Pentagon and the National Aeronautics and Space Administration—the people who put a man on the moon. This group correlates its work with that done by climate scientists all over the world. Together, these experts reference temperature readings and natural weather variations based on data collected worldwide since the 1880s, using thousands of thermometers and other sensors on everything from balloons and buoys to ships, aircraft, and even satellites. They look at atmospheric concentrations of carbon pollution going back 50 years and ice samples that attest to carbon levels in our atmosphere reaching back hundreds of thousands of years. And they track global fossil fuel consumption that is carefully monitored by government and industry as the basis for tax and royalty payments.

We know what's happening to our atmosphere. It contains more carbon dioxide than at any other time in at least 800,000 years. At 400 parts per million, the carbon dioxide content in our atmosphere is 43 percent higher than when we began burning fossil fuels in earnest with the dawn of the Industrial Revolution two centuries ago. Over the past decade, we've packed an additional 2.1 parts per million of carbon pollution, on average, into our atmosphere every year. That's three times as much as when daily measurements began nearly six decades ago.

Carbon dioxide is what scientists call a "greenhouse gas." Methane, the chief constituent in natural gas, is an even stronger greenhouse gas than carbon dioxide. In our atmosphere, such gases trap the sun's heat, much like a greenhouse does, contributing to the warming of the planet. Without any greenhouse gases, our planet would be too cold to support life. The amount of carbon dioxide we have pumped into the atmosphere by burning fossil fuels, however, has tipped the scale in the other direction: it's heating up the planet. To avert catastrophe, we need to get our hand off the scale.

"Climate change is occurring, is very likely caused primarily by the emission of greenhouse gases from human activities, and poses significant risks for a range of human and natural systems. Emissions continue to increase, which will result in further change and greater risks. Responding to those risks is a crucial challenge facing the United States and the world today and for many decades to come."

That's the conclusion of the National Academy of Sciences, which was chartered by the U.S. Congress in 1863 to report the bedrock truth about our natural world, as best as can possibly be discerned. It is our national scientific brain trust, and the conclusion above comes straight from the Academy's 2011 report, *America's Climate Choices*. The report is the product of hundreds of peer-reviewed analyses and studies. It was put together under the auspices of twenty-two senior scholars in their field, from institutions like Duke University, Stanford, Michigan State, Princeton, Georgia Tech, and the Massachusetts Institute of Technology.

When I hear people say they're not convinced climate change is happening, I ask myself what exactly it is they're waiting for. It can't possibly be more information.

Of the scientists who make their living studying what's happening to our climate, 97 percent agree that our planet is warming and the most important reason why is that we're dumping carbon pollution from burning fossil fuels into our atmosphere at a rate our natural systems can neither absorb nor tolerate. In fact, the consensus is even stronger than that.

In 2012, James Lawrence Powell, executive director of the National Physical Science Consortium, looked at 13,950 peer-reviewed scholarly articles on global climate. Powell wanted to find out how many of those authors reject the view that carbon pollution is causing the planet to warm, what Powell and others call "man-made global warming." The answer: 24. In other words, for every 581 scholars who published their findings about global climate conditions, just 1 rejected the reality of man-made climate change.

Powell is a serious scholar of national repute. He's the former president of Reed College and of the Los Angeles County Museum of Natural History. He served for 12 years on the National Science Board—appointed first by President Ronald Reagan and later by President George H. W. Bush. He's a Kentucky native with a bachelor's degree in geology who later earned his PhD in geochemistry from the Massachusetts Institute of Technology.

In early 2014, Powell updated his research. This time, he searched for scholarship on global climate published after his previous study. He found 9,136 peer-reviewed climate articles published in scientific journals worldwide between November 2012 and the end of December 2013. Only one article rejected the findings that we're cooking the planet with carbon. The dissenting view was published in the *Herald of the Russian Academy of Sciences*.

The fact is, we know what's happening to our climate. And this is what we know.

GLOBAL TEMPERATURES ARE RISING

In a little more than a hundred years, the Earth's average temperature has risen by about 1.4 degrees Fahrenheit, an increase of 2.5 percent. When it comes to average global temperatures, seemingly small differences can mean a lot. During the last Ice Age, when half of the American continent was covered in ice sheets up to a mile-and-a-half thick, temperatures ranged between 9 and 14 degrees Fahrenheit cooler than they are today. The warming that followed completely reshaped our world, but it did so over a period of 15,000 years.

Unless we reduce our use of fossil fuels, we're going to drive up average global temperatures by the end of this century to somewhere between 3 and 8 degrees Fahrenheit above where we were just a century ago. That would be the most rapid warming our Earth has experienced—by far—since the dinosaurs disappeared 65 million years ago. The results would be devastating: rising sea level swamps low-lying cities in coastal regions from Mexico to Madagascar; malnutrition puts hundreds of millions of climate refugees to flight in a crisis that threatens border integrity and global security; deserts expand from Somalia to China, while wet regions become wetter; tropical cyclones and other storms become more frequent and more intense; deadly heat waves become the norm across the Mediterranean, North Africa, and much of the United States; water scarcity intensifies across the Middle East, Africa, and the American West; species biodiversity plunges into full collapse.

It's staggering to think we are even capable, through human activity, of altering global climate on that scale. And yet, that is exactly what we are doing.

"Continued emissions of greenhouse gases will cause further warming and changes in all components of the climate system," the 2013 report from the Intergovernmental Panel on Climate Change stated. "Limiting climate change will require substantial and sustained reductions of greenhouse gas emissions."

The IPCC was formed in 1988 by two agencies of the United Nations—the UN Environment Programme and the World Meteorological Organization. Its 2013 assessment is the most authoritative and comprehensive scientific review of global climate change ever undertaken. It was produced by 859 authors and editors representing more than three dozen countries. It draws on peer-reviewed scientific literature and cites more than 9,200 documents. And the conclusions reflect a staggering 54,677 comments from nearly 1,100 expert reviewers worldwide. This is the most definitive agreement ever on a conservative estimate of what is happening to our world and the fossil fuel consumption that is driving the change.

When it comes to measuring and documenting what's happening in our world, there are few instruments more trustworthy than the thermometer. Galileo made one in 1592, and we've been improving them ever since. We know how to take the world's temperature. That's how we know the 15 hottest years on record, globally, have all occurred since 1997. Nine out of the ten hottest years ever have all occurred since 2002. Average global temperatures during June 2014 set an all-time high for that month, as did global temperatures in May 2014. June 2014 marked the 352nd consecutive month in which global temperatures were above the 20th century average. The last time global temperatures fell below the global average for the month of June was in 1976—the year Jimmy Carter was elected president.

Who says so? The National Climatic Data Center at the National Oceanic and Atmospheric Administration. This is the gold standard for global and U.S. climate data. Anyone who wants to know the facts can find current climate data on its website.

In the continental United States, the hottest year on record was 2012, when the mercury soared 3.26 degrees Fahrenheit above the 20th century average. The worst drought since the Dust Bowl hammered corn and soybean farmers and cattle ranchers from the Rocky Mountains to the Ohio River Valley. The Mississippi River got so low in places barges ran aground. Wildfires gorged on dry timber and fields, destroying more than two thousand homes and burning enough acreage to cover Connecticut and New Jersey combined. A summer derecho sent a train of storms barreling out of the Midwest all the way to the East Coast, killing at least 28 people. Hurricane Sandy killed 159 more.

All told, these disasters cost the country $139 billion, the U.S. insurance industry estimated, and taxpayers picked up the bulk of the tab. A 2013 NRDC analysis found that the U.S. government spent about $96 billion covering damages from these climate-related disasters—an average of $1,100 per taxpayer. That was more than our federal government spent on education, transportation, veterans benefits, or any other category of non-defense spending outside of Social Security, Medicare, and Medicaid.

No single weather event can be blamed exclusively on climate change. A changing climate, though, has become the stage our weather plays itself out on, and warmer temperatures have set that stage for more extreme weather.

Heat, after all, is energy. As our atmosphere is pumped up with more energy, our storms have the potential to pack a greater wallop. The warmer air gets the more moisture it holds, meaning weather systems bring more precipitation in wet regions where moisture accumulates.

Both of those factors were at work when Hurricane Sandy lambasted the Northeast with torrential rains, high winds, and a record storm surge, leaving at least $65 billion worth of destruction in its wake. The storm forced power outages for 8.5 million and swamped coastal areas with between one and nine feet of water from Florida to Maine. Hurricanes are nature's way of converting energy into wind. They're the result of complicated natural systems and their interaction with each other. And, as with any single weather event, no one is claiming that climate change caused Hurricane Sandy.

This much, though, is beyond dispute. These kinds of storms can gather energy from warm ocean waters. Sandy spent most of its time over Atlantic waters that were between 3 and 6 degrees Fahrenheit above the 30-year average for that time of year. That allowed the storm to intensify, because, as it lingered over the warm Atlantic waters, Sandy absorbed energy and moisture, so that when it hit, it delivered a punishing blow.

People who say we can't afford to take action against climate change have got it wrong. The truth is, we can't afford not to act, or we'll be spending more and more to cope with one climate-related disaster after the next and to build in resistance to and resilience against the impacts of this worsening crisis. Mayors, governors, and other leaders around the country are already investing in ways to make their communities more resilient in the face of extreme weather events, but we need to do much more to become stronger and better prepared for the next superstorm, the next drought, the next heat wave.

"A CRISIS WE CAN'T AFFORD TO IGNORE . . ."

One such disaster is creeping upon us by degrees, but drawing nearer with each high tide.

As oceans warm, their waters expand, contributing to rising sea level. Global sea level has risen about eight inches since 1880, when reliable record keeping began. That, though, is a global figure. Since about 1990, the sea level along the Eastern Seaboard, from Cape Hatteras, North Carolina to just north of Boston, Massachusetts, has been rising three or four times faster than the global rate, the U.S. Geological Survey—the nation's official bearer of Earth science data—reported in June 2012. That area includes several U.S. military installations, including U.S. Naval Station Norfolk, the largest navy base in the world. Over the past century, the sea level has risen a foot and a half at Norfolk, putting the base at growing risk of flooding during storms and raising long-term strategic concerns over the future of the home port of the Atlantic Fleet. "Sea level rise acts as a threat multiplier, generating more intense storms and leading to an increase in both mission impairment and duration," states a June 2014 assessment by the U.S. Army Corps of Engineers titled "Quantifing Coastal Storm and Sea Level Rise Risks to Naval Station Norfolk."

Coastal property owners are getting a similar message. In 2003, the National Flood Insurance Program—a government-backed indemnity program—provided coverage for just under $700 million worth of property nationwide. As of May 2014, that figure had risen to a staggering $1.3 trillion, the second-largest U.S. government liability after Social Security.

Most climate experts believe sea level is on track to rise by somewhere between one and four feet by the end of the century. This means that a storm surge will rise higher, putting more buildings and other property at risk during hurricanes, high winds, and heavy rains. An increase near the higher end of the projections, moreover, would put much of Miami underwater, including existing property currently worth up to $208 billion, according to estimates by the Risky Business Project. By 2100, the group estimates, up to $1.4 trillion worth of existing coastal property, from the Gulf Coast to the northern reaches of the Eastern Seaboard, could be below sea level or at risk during high tides.

"If we stay on our current path, some homes and commercial properties with 30-year mortgages in places like Virginia, North Carolina, New Jersey, Alabama, Florida and Louisiana and elsewhere could quite literally be underwater before the note is paid off," the group reported in June 2014.

Co-chaired by former New York City Mayor Michael Bloomberg, former U.S. Treasury Secretary Henry Paulson Jr., and former venture capitalist Tom Steyer, the Risky Business Project seeks to assess the long-term financial risks of global climate change. Those risks, the group concluded, are both substantial and growing.

"The American economy faces multiple and significant risks from climate change," the group stated in its report. "Staying on our current path will only increase our exposure."

As the group's name makes clear, the Risky Business Project is focused on a cold-eyed assessment of the very real prospects for serious economic damage due to climate change. And they're telling us that we're ignoring the imminent and growing risks of climate change at our peril.

"This is a crisis we can't afford to ignore," Paulson wrote in the *Times*. "I feel as if I'm watching as we fly in slow motion on a collision course toward a giant mountain. We can see the crash coming, and yet we're sitting on our hands rather than altering course."

The Risky Business report spotlighted the danger of sea-level rise, but that isn't the only hazard facing the oceans. The same carbon pollution that is heating the planet is also changing the chemical composition of the world's oceans, making them increasingly acidic in ways that threaten the entire life system of our seas.

Our oceans absorb about one-fourth of the carbon dioxide released into the atmosphere. The resulting rise in acidity reduces the amount of calcium carbonate minerals in the water. Oysters, clams, coral, and other species depend on these minerals to produce skeletons and shells. Rising acidification is disrupting those critical functions, creating what some have called "osteoporosis of the sea," impeding the ability of many marine animals to grow properly, reproduce, or, in the case of coral, replenish natural reefs.

Among the richest repositories of natural species diversity on Earth, coral reefs provide essential habitat for about 25 percent of all marine species. They in turn, are food for other species up the chain, including the roughly 1 billion people worldwide who depend on seafood as their chief source of protein. The carbon pollution from our dependence on fossil fuels is threatening the health of the world's oceans and all they support. As someone who has always loved the sea, I find it painful to imagine a world without mussels or beaches without shells.

When it comes to monitoring climate change, the canary in the coal mine is ice, the massive global glaciers, sheets, permanent snow, and sea ice that together lock up seven of every ten gallons of freshwater on Earth. As global temperatures rise, much of that ice is melting, releasing huge volumes of water that, in the case of land-based ice, can't help but send sea levels rising further, to potentially catastrophic levels.

In October 2011, scientists with the National Atmospheric and Space Administration spotted a crack in the massive Pine Island Glacier in western Antarctica. Over the next two years, the rift widened, and, in November of 2013, an iceberg 11 times the size of Manhattan and 200 feet thick sheared off and began drifting across the Amundsen Sea and toward open ocean.

Scientists with the National Atmospheric and Space Administration closely tracked it, not only because rogue icebergs adrift in open waters pose a hazard to ships and crew, but also because the half-dozen massive glaciers that feed the Amundsen Sea are melting faster than any other ice anywhere in Antarctica. There's enough water locked up in the Amundsen glaciers to raise global sea level four feet. That ice is melting, NASA scientists say, and it isn't going to stop.

"We've passed the point of no return," said glaciologist Ed Rignot, senior research scientist with NASA's Jet Propulsion Laboratory, which uses satellite imagery to track the condition of major ice sheets globally, and a professor of Earth System Science at the University of California, Irvine. "At this point it's just a matter of time before these glaciers completely disappear to sea," he said in a May 2014 video posted on the NASA website. At the present rate of melting, he said, "They would disappear completely in a couple of centuries."

That may sound like a long time. But if those glaciers melt over the next 200 years, they would release enough water to raise global sea level by a quarter of an inch per year—on top of the sea level rise already projected.

Meanwhile, another great sheet of ice is melting at an alarming rate. Seven percent of the Earth's fresh water is locked up in Greenland, in a massive sheet of ancient ice an average of 1.4 miles thick and spread out over an area roughly the size of Alaska. Currently, this ice is melting, releasing anywhere between 27 trillion and 68 trillion gallons of water a year into North Atlantic and Arctic waters. Even at the lower end of that scale, that's enough to put half the state of Texas under a foot of water. If the Greenland ice sheet were to melt completely, NASA calculates, it would drive up global sea level by 23 feet. At that point, London is Venice, Venice is gone, and we'll need scuba gear to visit New Orleans.

There is another kind of ice that climate scientists are watching just as closely: Arctic sea ice is vanishing before our eyes.

At the end of the summer of 1980, Arctic sea ice covered three million square miles, roughly the size of the continental United

States. At the end of the summer of 2012, 56 percent of that ice was gone. In effect, we'd lost, in that time, enough sea ice to cover a little more than half of the country.

How do we know? The same NASA lab that tracks ice in Antarctica monitors Arctic sea ice, using sophisticated microwave sensors in satellites that capture more than a dozen images over the region every day. Arctic sea ice recovers in winter, and more ice melts in some summers than others. The summer of 2012 was a record low for Arctic sea ice. Measurements taken at the end of each summer melt season, though, show a consistent pattern over time. We're losing this ice far faster in summer than it can recover in winter.

Arctic sea ice plays a critical role in moderating global climate, acting like a mirror to reflect back into space about 80 percent of the sunlight that strikes it. As the ice melts in summer, the equation shifts. Dark ocean water absorbs 90 percent of the sunlight, warming the ocean. Because it is frozen seawater floating in the ocean, Arctic ice doesn't raise global sea level when it melts. As that sea ice disappears, though, the ocean becomes warmer, putting the remaining ice at growing risk.

The sea ice is telling us in no uncertain terms, our climate is warming on a global scale.

I didn't have to see it for myself to believe it, but gazing up at the edge of an ice sheet twelve stories high from the Arctic waters off the Norwegian archipelago of Svalbard one summer changed forever my view of ice and its role in our natural systems. Svalbard—the Viking word for "cold coast"—is a group of mountainous islands halfway between the Arctic Circle and the North Pole. About 60 percent of the land is covered by permanent snow and glaciers, some of which press to the edge of the sea. I traveled there by ship in July 2008 with a group that included former President Jimmy Carter, John Carr of the U.S. Conference of Catholic Bishops, and Julian Dowdswell, director of the Scott Polar Research Institute at Cambridge. We'd come to learn more about climate change and its impact on the Arctic. Our journey had brought us within several hundred yards of one of the largest ice sheets on Earth.

"If we had been here ten years ago, where would that ice have been," I asked Dowdswell, one of the world's foremost experts on the subject. "It would have been," he replied, "right where you are now."

"THIS IS AN OPPORTUNITY"

Of all the science, all the trend lines, all the economic analysis and portents of peril, sometimes the best way for us to comprehend what is at stake here is simply to go outside and look around, because the Earth is telling us in every way it can that we are baking climate chaos into our children's future.

Farmers are our nation's first conservationists. They live and work close to the land. They understand fresh water, clean air, and the eternal connection between the health of our natural systems and the welfare of our people. They note the passage of one season into the next.

From the time he was a boy on his parents' Iowa farm, Matt Russell knew hot summers, big storms, and the odd dusting of snow in springtime. Lately, though, he's noticed that extreme weather has become the norm.

In 2008, torrential rains inundated Iowa farms with the kind of flood planners expect once every 500 years. Epic floods again washed out crops in each of the next two years. In 2012, Iowa pastureland dried to dust, and corn and soybeans withered in the nation's worst drought since the Dust Bowl. Then, in 2013, that foot of snow in early May combined with heavy rains to give Iowa its wettest spring on record, leaving farmers like Matt with $2 billion in crop losses.

When that kind of calamity befalls you and your neighbors in the space of just six years, he said, you don't have to be an environmental activist to figure out something's amiss.

"The scientists have been telling us what climate change looks like and, as farmers, we're living it," Matt explained to NRDC staffers who visited his Coyote Run Farm near Lacona, Iowa, in March 2014. "If you ask any farmer, they may not want to engage you on the politics of climate change. But if you start talking to them about weather, they're going to tell you it's a different ballgame."

In fact, explained Matt, who is the coordinator of the State Food Policy Project at Drake University's agricultural law center, some farmers across the state are starting to wonder how long their children will be able to make a living off the land given the ravages of heat, drought and flood that have whipsawed their region in recent years.

"We're already experiencing the effects of climate change," Matt told a group gathered on a spring afternoon to discuss the issue at the Bethesda Lutheran Church in Ames. "It's going to be very difficult for us to continue to feed a growing population if the agricultural systems that we have in place now are no longer viable with climate that's changed."

Like American farmers down through all time, Matt vests faith in the future. Hardly one to wring his hands, he sees opportunity amid challenge, and he understand the urgency of acting now. Farmers, he said, can be part of the solution, helping to foster the innovation and investment we need to reduce our reliance on fossil fuels, protect the natural systems we all depend on, and develop farming practices that help to reduce the carbon dioxide in our atmosphere and lock it away instead in our forests and fields.

"This is an opportunity for American farmers to lead the world in what it needs, and we can do that in a way that makes our farms stronger, more sustainable, more resilient and more profitable," Matt said over the phone in August 2014. "This is our generational opportunity, and if we miss it it'll be the first generation of American farmers who haven't risen to the occasion, if we don't step up on climate change."

We cannot turn our backs on people like Matt Russell. His challenge is our challenge, as his opportunity is ours. We can't ignore all that, just as we can't walk away from our obligation to protect future generations from the dangers of climate change. In the long years I've called for action to cut the carbon pollution that's driving climate chaos, I've never been more driven than I am now, and that drive is now coupled with some increasing optimism. We've arrived at a hopeful moment. People like Matt are part of the reason why.

We have a new generation of American stewards who understand the urgency of needed change. We have a widening circle of business leaders who understand the historic opportunity to create a cleaner, more sustainable, and more resilient world. And we have leadership in the White House that understands the stakes for our future. Together, these three forces can change the world. We must all be a part of that change.

SIX

Containing Carbon

There are some problems so long in the making and so complex that they can't be solved overnight or through any one magical measure or act. What we're sometimes called upon to do is to manage those kinds of problems, prevent them from spreading, and keep them from getting worse while we make the progress we can to set the stage for a fuller resolution over time. That way, we can steadily diminish the impact of a problem while we work to develop the comprehensive solutions we know we'll need to put it behind us once and for all.

Global climate change has been centuries in the making. We've been dumping dangerous carbon pollution into the Earth's atmosphere at a rapidly accelerating rate since the dawn of the Industrial Revolution. We're not going to turn that around overnight. What we must do, is contain the spread of carbon pollution, keep the problem from getting worse, then reduce it outright.

This is a global problem, it will require a global solution, but it begins, right here, at home. The United States pumped 5.4 billion tons of carbon pollution into the atmosphere in 2013, about 15 percent of the world total. About 70 percent of U.S. carbon emissions come from three sources: our power plants, cars, and trucks. Any serious plan to reduce our carbon footprint must address those sources. That's exactly what we're doing as part of Obama's comprehensive climate action plan that President Obama announced in June 2013.

Progress will take time, but the urgency of a changing climate and its serious worldwide implications must drive the action. The president's plan faces stubborn opposition from the formidable forces of the fossil fuels industry. The president, though, is on the right side of history. It's on our generation to begin the transformation that will contain carbon and set the country on the path to reducing our reliance on oil, gas, and coal, for the sake of our nation's future prosperity, security, and strength.

After four decades on the front lines of environmental advocacy, I'm convinced that climate change is the central challenge of our time for the protection of the natural systems we depend on, for our progress, our well-being, and our very survival. Taking action to protect future generations against the dangers of climate change is job number one for me. It has been for decades and will remain so, I expect, for as long as I have breath to speak. The task we face is to build the national consensus for action, to build the national momentum for change. That overarching goal has galvanized a nationwide community of environmental leaders, activists, and supporters. It has united us with a growing body of business executives, investors, labor organizers, entrepreneurs, faith leaders, and health experts who fully grasp the urgent need to act and can see the world of opportunity that awaits us as we do. And it has energized a president who understands the stakes for our country.

"NOT JUST TO OURSELVES, BUT TO ALL POSTERITY"

Just before noon on January 21, 2013, I joined cabinet secretaries, members of Congress, and scores of other dignitaries in temporary bleachers at the U.S. Capitol, where we watched President Obama be sworn in for a second term. In lofty prose and eloquent speech, he harkened back to our history just enough to remind us of who we are, as a broadly diverse group of Americans, and then he laid out a vision of where we must go, united together as one. He spoke of restoring economic might and ending war, of responsibility and resilience, quiet dignity, inner strength. And he talked about the moral duty we have, one generation to the next, to leave this land to our children in even better shape than it was left for us.

"We, the people, still believe that our obligations as Americans are not just to ourselves, but to all posterity," the president said. "We will respond to the threat of climate change, knowing that a failure to do so would betray our children and future generations."

I will never forget the rousing ovation that greeted that pledge, a roar of support that welled up from the steps of our nation's Capitol, stretched out the length and breadth of our National Mall, and reached into the living rooms and kitchens of Americans all across this country.

The following year, in June of 2014, President Obama made good on his pledge, rolling out what he called his "Clean Power Plan," a proposal to cut carbon emissions from power plants, our single largest source of the dangerous industrial carbon pollution that is driving climate chaos.

Under the president's plan, we will reduce the carbon pollution from our existing power plants by 26 percent by 2020—when compared to 2005 levels—and by 30 percent, in total, by 2030. That will keep 730 million tons of carbon pollution out of our atmosphere annually, as much as is kicked out by 150 million automobiles. In other words, we would have to park two-thirds of the cars in America—permanently—to reduce our carbon pollution by this much.

Through Obama's plan, we'll achieve those reductions in a way that puts states in the driver's seat and gives utility companies and consumers the flexibility they need to get the job done in the most cost-effective way possible. And we'll do it in a way that strengthens our economy, creates jobs, makes our workers more competitive, pays up to a dollar's worth of benefits for every dime that we invest, and strikes a blow against the central environmental challenge of our time. At NRDC, our analysis shows that this plan could be even more ambitious, could do even more to protect our future from climate change, could do even more to roll back the dangerous carbon pollution that threatens our world. The president's plan, though, lays the groundwork for what we must do: contain the spread of carbon pollution, keep the problem from getting worse, then gradually reduce it outright. And we will continue to advocate for even stronger actions.

Right now, in this country, about 1,500 power plants fired by fossil fuels account for nearly 40 percent of our carbon footprint, with the largest share of that coming from aging units that burn coal. And yet, astonishingly, there are no limits on how much of this dangerous carbon pollution these plants may dump into our air. That has to change, and we are beginning down that path.

After all, we limit the pollutants these plants release that cause deadly soot and smog, as well as toxins like mercury. It's time we set commonsense limits on the carbon pollution that is cooking our planet and imperiling our future. That's what the president's Clean Power Plan will do.

Under this plan, the U.S. Environmental Protection Agency articulates the national goal: reducing carbon pollution today so our children don't inherit climate chaos tomorrow. That seems simple and clear enough.

"By leveraging cleaner energy sources and cutting energy waste, this plan will clean the air we breathe while helping slow climate change so we can leave a safe and healthy future for our kids," EPA administrator Gina McCarthy explained when she announced the plan. "Our action will sharpen America's competitive edge, spur innovation, and create jobs."

Before coming to the EPA, McCarthy served in both Republican and Democratic administrations at the state level. She has been a tenacious and fair-minded leader, crossing the country on listening tours to ensure she hears a full range of views on curbing carbon pollution.

The EPA plan gives each state a reduction target tailored to its own unique energy mix. That way, a state like, say, Kentucky, which is heavily reliant on coal for its electricity, can contribute to the national goal by cutting its carbon footprint by a smaller overall percentage than a state like, say, Virginia, which gets much less of its total power from coal-fired plants. In both cases, we can reduce the intensity of carbon pollution, in a way that helps to reduce our carbon footprint nationwide.

Each state, then, develops its own plan for meeting its target, working closely with the power companies that serve that state. Each state's plan must satisfy the requirements of EPA, or the agency will step in and design a plan that does. And power companies have the flexibility they need to hit the target in the most cost-effective way.

There are four basic baskets of options available for them: promoting energy efficiency; investing in wind, solar, or other forms of renewable power that don't produce carbon pollution; shifting their generating mix toward lower-carbon options; and tuning up existing power plants for maximum efficiency. Each option, or a mix of any or all of those options, offers unique benefits and opportunities for utility companies and consumers.

The cleanest and cheapest way to shrink our carbon footprint is to reduce the amount of electricity we waste. That's why we at NRDC see energy efficiency as the cornerstone of this plan. Power companies can go a long way toward meeting their carbon reduction goals by providing incentives to help families and businesses make the improvements needed to do more with less electricity and save money on the electric bills in our homes and workplaces. The cleanest and cheapest way to shrink our carbon footprint is to reduce the amount of electricity we waste, and the potential for savings is huge.

How much can we save using a plan like the one the president proposed? To find out, NRDC hired one of the top consulting firms in the world, ICF International. Since its founding in 1969, ICF has grown into a global powerhouse with 4,500 employees in 70 offices worldwide. Its clients include industry and government entities like the U.S. Census Bureau, the Department of Homeland Security, and the Pentagon.

NRDC believes we can cut the power sector's carbon footprint even further than the president's plan provides. We asked ICF to analyze a plan to cut carbon emissions in the power sector by 38 percent by 2025. Based on that approach, somewhat more aggressive than what the president has proposed, ICF found that we can save, as a nation, $37.4 billion per year on electricity costs by using this proposal to advance energy efficiency investments.

It works out to a savings of $24.3 billion per year for our businesses, and $13 billion for our homes—or, on average, $103 per year in savings for the typical American household.

Homeowners can reduce waste, and save money, by taking prudent steps like replacing old windows and beefing up insulation, modernizing heating and air conditioning systems, and replacing aging dishwashers, refrigerators, water heaters, and the like with newer, energy-efficient appliances. In many leading states, public service commissions have long required power companies to provide incentives and other assistance to help their customers save energy. The companies are allowed to recover the costs of those incentives through their rates. But that's cheaper—for the power company and its consumers—than building expensive new power plants.

In addition to the electricity savings, investing in energy efficiency will create jobs—274,000 of them nationwide, IFC International found—as demand increases for roofers, carpenters, electricians and other workers needed to help improve the efficiency of our workplaces and homes.

The second option for power companies is to invest in wind turbines, solar panels or other renewable energy sources that don't produce carbon pollution. How realistic is that? It's already happening on a large scale. During the three-year period covering 2011–2013, wind and solar installations accounted for 44 percent of all the new electricity-generating capacity in our nation. That was about three times the amount of new coal-fired capacity, according to the Federal Energy Regulatory Commission, which tracks new plant construction.

In the first half of 2014, wind and solar provided 5.5 percent of our electricity nationally—more than ten times the level of 2005. As that percentage continues to climb, our carbon footprint will shrink. And, here again, we're talking about job creation. There were nearly 200,000 Americans working to build wind turbines and solar energy systems as of the beginning of 2014. Those industries, which barely existed by comparison just a decade ago, are poised for additional growth as we get serious about reducing carbon pollution from our power plants and put in place policies, like the president's plan, to help.

The third option for utility companies is to shift their generating mix toward lower-carbon sources. Power plants fueled by natural gas, for example, provided 27 percent of our electricity, nationally, in 2013—up from 19 percent in 2005. Natural gas is no panacea for our carbon woes. It's a fossil fuel. Producing it is putting many communities, families, and resources at risk. Many natural gas production and distribution operations leak prodigious amounts of methane and other pollutants. Burning gas produces carbon pollution. So we need to stop the leaks, ensure current plants run as efficiently as possible, and minimize our reliance on natural gas. Gas does burn cleaner than coal. So, to the extent that electricity generated by gas-fired turbines replaces power from coal, one result can be a reduction in carbon emissions from power production. Dollar for dollar, though, investing in efficiency and renewable power are by far the better options and the pathway to a carbon-free future.

Finally, utility companies may choose to tune up their generators for maximum efficiency so they produce more power from whatever fuel they do burn and to prioritize getting the most productivity possible out of current plants rather than rushing to build new ones. That, too, can reduce the amount of carbon pollution emitted from the smokestack. And, of course, utilities can employ any combination of these options that suits them, so long as the result is lower carbon emissions.

"This plan is all about flexibility," Administrator McCarthy told reporters when she rolled out the proposal on June 2, 2014. "That's what makes it ambitious but also achievable. That's how we keep our energy affordable and reliable," she said. "The glue that holds this plan together, and the key to making it work, is that each state's goal is tailored to its own circumstances, and states have the flexibility to reach their goal in whatever way works best for them."

BREATHING EASIER

As each state moves closer to curbing its carbon pollution, it will also help improve the health of its residents, because the steps we take to cut our carbon emissions can also reduce other kinds of pollution that contribute to the formation of soot and smog. And those pollutants increase the risk of asthma attacks, heart disease, and even lung cancer.

"Carbon pollution from power plants come packaged with dangerous pollutants like particulate matter, nitrogen oxide and sulfur dioxide, and they put our children and our families at even more risk," Administrator McCarthy explained. "This is about protecting our health."

The EPA calculates, in fact, that cutting back the carbon pollution from our power plants, in the way this plan provides, will reduce the pollutants that cause both soot and smog by more than 25 percent, with big benefits starting to show up in 2020. That means real health benefits for our people. By reducing those pollutants, the EPA estimates, we will avoid between 2,700 and 6,600 premature deaths a year by 2030. We'll prevent up to 150,000 asthma attacks in children—annually. We'll reduce heart attacks—by as many as 3,300 a year. And our people will clock nearly half-a-million work days each year they might otherwise have missed due to poor health.

"It's going to result in lower medical bills, fewer trips to the emergency room, especially for those most vulnerable: those kids, especially those kids that have asthma, our elderly and our infirm," said McCarthy. "This is also about environmental justice, because lower-income families and communities of color are hardest hit."

That message came through loud and clear in July 2014 polling that found that 62 percent of American minorities feel not enough is being done to address the dangers of climate change. The survey, performed by the polling outfit Brilliant Strategies for NRDC and several other organizations that make up the advocacy group Green for All, queried 800 African American and Latino likely voters in

Florida, Michigan, Ohio, and six other states. By an overwhelming margin—70 percent—minority voters are more likely to support a political candidate willing to expand resources to address the issue and help grow the jobs that come with that investment than for a candidate who claims taking action against climate change will somehow hurt economic growth.

It's difficult to put a price tag on averting illness or death in favor of improved health. The EPA, though, estimates that the climate and public health benefits of reducing carbon pollution from our power plants will be worth between $55 billion and $93 billion a year, with much of the impact beginning in 2020, while the investment required to clean up those plants will range from $7.3 billion to $8.8 billion by 2030. In other words, we could realize upward of $90 billion in annual benefits from a program that costs less than a tenth that amount.

The Clean Air Act is the key to delivering these benefits. NRDC has been working to advance action against climate change for decades, and we've been eyeing the Clean Air Act as a vehicle for action for years, under the leadership of our stellar climate trio, David Doniger, Dave Hawkins, and, until the spring of 2014, Dan Lashof.

Doniger and Hawkins, between the two of them, have more than eighty years of experience with the Clean Air Act. Both have served stints with the Environmental Protection Agency. Doniger was a senior clean air attorney, and Hawkins penned much of the body of regulations in the 1970s that limit the amount of soot and smog in the air we breathe. Lashof, who has a PhD in energy and natural resources, also came to NRDC from EPA and is one of the nation's foremost experts on the science of climate change. In 2014, he left NRDC to head up climate change advocacy as chief operation officer at NextGen Climate.

Together, these three understood that the Clean Air Act gives the president the authority, and the obligation, to put in place commonsense standards that limit the amount of dangerous carbon pollution from our cars, power plants, and other large industries. This authority has withstood one challenge after the next from the fossil fuel industry before the U.S. Supreme Court.

In 2007 the Court decided in *Massachusetts v. EPA* that the Clean Air Act gives the EPA the authority to set carbon pollution standards for motor vehicles. In 2001, the Court held in *American Electric Power v. Connecticut* that the EPA can do the same for new and existing power plants. And in June 2014, in *Utility Air Regulatory*

Group v. EPA, the Court ruled that the core provision of the Clean Air Act's permitting requirements also apply to carbon pollution. In other words, the Court has made it emphatically clear that the EPA has an obligation, under the Clean Air Act, to set emission standards that limit the amount of carbon pollution that can be dumped into the atmosphere by cars, power plants, and other big industries.

We at NRDC, along with our environmental colleagues, supported the comprehensive clean energy and climate legislation that passed in the House of Representatives in 2009. That bill called for meaningful reductions in carbon pollution, and it provided resources and incentives to help promote the investments in efficiency and renewable power that can help to get us there. When partisan gridlock and fossil fuel influence bogged down the legislation in the Senate, I was more than deeply disappointed. I was angry, because I believed then, as I do now, that our political system responded to special interests in a way that failed the broader national interest. Because of that, we've squandered five years that were critical to addressing the climate crisis. But make no mistake, Congress vested the president with the authority to act on his own to protect future generations against the dangers of climate change when it passed the Clean Air Act in 1970. The law gave the president this authority, the Supreme Court has affirmed it—three times—and we're moving forward.

The Clean Air Act also gives all stakeholders the opportunity to weigh in on how best to structure individual state plans for cutting carbon pollution. States have until the end of June 2016, to submit their plans for EPA approval. That allows two years, in other words, for each state to develop its own individual approach to reducing our overall carbon footprint. Many states will qualify for extensions of up to two years, meaning they could have until 2018 to complete a plan for meeting their carbon reduction goals by 2030.

The president's plan accounts for differences in each state's energy mix. It lets utilities choose the most cost-efficient way to hit the target. It makes our air safer to breathe. It creates American jobs. It lowers our electricity bills. It strikes a blow against the central environmental challenge of our time. And we can make it even stronger.

Small wonder, then, that 70 percent of the American public supports the plan, according to a June 2014 poll by *The Washington Post* and ABC News. A similar poll by *The Wall Street Journal* and NBC News put the support level at 67 percent, with 57 percent saying they would back the proposal even if it resulted in higher utility bills.

"President Obama made the right decision," the *Miami Herald* wrote in an editorial backing the proposal. "The most important aspect of the Obama plan is that it represents, at last, a concrete response to an undeniable challenge," continued the *Herald* ,one of dozens of papers to endorse the plan. "Doing nothing is not an option when facing the dire consequences of climate change. Human beings are not helpless when it comes to protecting themselves, their planet and the future."

Even in the capital of the coa- producing state of West Virginia, the *Charleston Gazette* stood up for the president's plan and decried its critics.

"Predictably, West Virginia conservatives went ballistic over the Obama administration's modest, reasonable attempt to reduce air pollution and curtail global warming caused by coal-burning power plants," read the *Gazette*'s June 2014 editorial. "As we've said before, instead of raging against pollution controls—or trying to score political points—West Virginia leaders should launch intelligent planning for the inevitable future when coal is gone."

The *Gazette* noted that industry trends, dwindling reserves of high-quality coal, and market factors—not environmental safeguards—had long since set the Mountain State's coal industry on a long-term course of decline. "Political ranting and posturing by conservatives won't solve anything. Instead, sensible leaders should focus on adapting West Virginia's economy to ongoing change that is unstoppable."

From coastal regions threatened by rising seas, to West Virginia's coal country, the public is calling for action. And yet, compelling as these voices are, we all knew who would oppose the plan: the fossil fuel industry and its political allies, the same special interests that have always cared more about protecting big-polluter profits than in standing up for our children's future.

Even before Obama unveiled his proposal, 29 members of the Texas congressional delegation signed a letter opposing the plan, claiming that it would drive up electricity rates, squeeze the economy, and curtail job growth in the Lone Star state.

Except that it won't.

There's more to that state's energy future than oil and gas. Texas, it turns out, leads the nation in power production from wind turbines, generating enough electricity from this zero-carbon, renewable source to power more than 3.3 million average American homes, the American Wind Energy Association reports. Texas may be the oil capital of the world, but it got 10 percent of its electricity from wind turbines in 2013, and that figure is growing. As to economic growth and jobs, there are at least 45 manufacturing facilities in Texas making turbines, blades, towers, and other components of wind generation gear. More than $23 billion has been invested in Texas wind projects. And farmers, ranchers, and other landowners there are receiving roughly $40 million a year in lease payments from wind turbine developers, money that is helping to keep the family ranch and farm alive in communities all across the Lone Star state.

The people of Texas, it appears, are about a generation ahead of those who purport to represent them in the U.S. Congress. The state is already making progress in reducing its carbon footprint, through a combination of energy efficiency codes for buildings and renewable energy goals. The president's plan will encourage those trends in ways that benefit all Americans—Texans included.

"Far from draconian, the plan gives states much flexibility in deciding how to reduce carbon emissions. Options include greater reliance on natural gas-fueled plants and wind, solar and nuclear-electric generation as well as using cap-and-trade systems to encourage energy producers to move to cleaner technologies," the *Houston Chronicle* wrote in an editorial in support of the plan. "As in the past, opponents are claiming the emissions restrictions will boost the price of electricity for everyone and damage the economy. They inflate cost estimates and ignore the already significant economic damage caused by rising temperatures and sea levels and the likelihood that the situation will drastically worsen in the coming decades if the status quo prevails."

The *Chronicle* assailed the Texas congressional delegation for its "knee-jerk opposition" to this proposal, adding that, "If members of Congress feel bypassed, they have only themselves to blame. Perhaps they should stop writing letters and start writing legislation to address the growing threat of climate change."

Congress, of course, was never bypassed. This plan began with Congress—four decades ago.

In 1970, with overwhelming support from members of both parties, Congress passed the Clean Air Act. Not one member of the U.S. Senate voted against it; just one member of the House of Representatives did. It was signed into law by President Richard Nixon and then strengthened two decades later under another Republican president, George H. W. Bush.

The Clean Air Act gives the president the authority, and the responsibility, to limit the dangerous carbon pollution that is driving climate change and imperiling our future. This builds on four decades of deliberate, methodical, commonsense safeguards. We already use the Clean Air Act to protect our health from sulfur, nitrogen, mercury, and soot from power plants. Its time to set limits on carbon pollution too. The Clean Air Act is the right tool for the job, as the Supreme Court has affirmed three times.

The Clean Air Act has been the target of constant legal challenges by big polluters pretty much since the day it was signed into law. At NRDC, we've devoted decades to defending this bedrock of clean air protections, so none of us was surprised when the usual critics—some of the nation's biggest polluters among them—came out of the woodwork to sow disinformation and doubt when it came time to take action against climate change. Some, like the U.S. Chamber of Commerce and its deep-pocketed members from the fossil fuel industry, sounded their tired old "Chicken Little" refrain, warning that we can't cut carbon pollution without collapsing our economy, just as they've done every single time we've done anything in this country to try to clean up our water, air, and lands or to create a healthier and more sustainable future for our children.

These same big-polluter interests warned of disaster when we got the lead out of our gasoline, reduced acid rain from our skies, and removed ozone-destroying chemicals out of our air conditioners. They were wrong every time—and they're wrong now.

In its first twenty years, the Clean Air Act provided the country with $22 trillion in health and other benefits—more than forty times the $500 billion invested during that period to clean up our air. We now have four decades of experience with the Clean Air Act, and here's what's going to happen. This plan is going to drive American innovation, investment and job creation. It's going to help clean up our air. And it's going to take a big bite out of our single largest source of the carbon pollution that's making climate change worse.

ADAPTING TO CHANGE

It's long past time for us to clean up the dangerous industrial carbon pollution from our nation's fossil-fuel-burning power plants. President Obama has laid out a way we can do that and get a return on our investment of up to tenfold.

Unfortunately, that's not good enough for the fossil fuel industry and its political allies on Capitol Hill. On the day the president laid out his plan, Senate Minority Leader Mitch McConnell, a Republican from the coal-producing state of Kentucky, called the proposal "a dagger in the heart of the American middle class, and to representative Democracy itself." Never mind that, in drafting its power plant carbon standards, the EPA largely adopted a 23-page document from Kentucky's energy department, urging that states be granted wide latitude in determining the best way to cut carbon pollution. McConnell introduced a bill to kill the president's carbon reduction proposal, calling it a "war on coal jobs."

Coal has played an important role throughout our country's history. It once powered the railroads that moved American passengers and commerce. It fired furnaces that forged iron and steel. Even today it fuels the power plants that produce nearly 40 percent of our electricity. But coal's long run is drawing to a close, and the transition is well underway. In 2000, more than 150 coal plants were on the drawing boards, but only 45 have come on line. Most have been cancelled as a result of shifting market forces and pressure from advocates like the Sierra Club's Beyond Coal campaign.

We have paid a high price for our use of coal, none more so than the coal miners themselves, far too many of whom have sacrificed their lives and health to bring us this fuel since the dawning of our industrial age. The rest of us have paid as well, with toxic pollutants that have damaged our health and carbon pollution that is cooking the planet. We have to turn that around.

The coal mining industry, meanwhile, is undergoing a transition driven chiefly by the forces of markets and mechanization.

It's been decades since legions of coal miners dominated the economies of states like Kentucky. As a source of jobs, the industry is in the mature stages of a long decline. A century ago there were more than 700,000 coal miners in the country. As of 2013 there were about 80,000, reports the U.S. Bureau of Labor Statistics.

The biggest part of the story has been mechanization, which has steadily cut the number of workers needed to mine a truckload of coal. That has combined with market shifts, as coal has struggled to compete with natural gas as a fuel for certain utility and industrial purposes. Those trends have been coupled with a shift toward increased strip mining of especially large sites, particularly in the western states, as many of the rich underground veins of high-quality Appalachian coal have become tapped out. Strip mining requires far fewer workers per ton of coal than underground mining does.

West of the Mississippi River, just 91 large mines produced 40 percent more coal in 2012 than the 1,126 mines east of the Mississippi, and they did so with 27 percent fewer miners, according to the

Energy Information Administration. In the first quarter of 2014, Wyoming alone produced more than twice as much coal as West Virginia, Kentucky, and Pennsylvania combined.

At the same time, the country's coal consumption has dropped 18 percent in just the past seven years, as coal-fired power plants, which are, on average, 42 years old nationwide, are out-competed by electricity generation plants powered by the wind, sun, or natural gas.

These market-based trends have nothing to do with the president's plan to reduce our nation's carbon pollution, but they are putting pressure on coal mining jobs, so let's be clear. There are 80,000 coal miners in America. There are about 200,000 Americans who get up every day and go to work building wind turbines and solar energy facilities according to data compiled by the American Wind Energy Association and the Solar Foundation, the authorities in their respective fields. And they are part of a corps of 3.4 million Americans who are working to create a more sustainable future for us all by building renewable power systems, developing the next generation of energy-efficient cars, homes, and workplaces or other activities categorized as "green jobs" by the U.S. Bureau of Labor Statistics, which has been the gold standard for American workforce data for more than a century.

Those 80,000 coal-mining jobs are important. The 3.4 million green jobs are important too. Those jobs are our future. The Clean Power Plan will help promote more of those jobs. We need to connect the opportunities of the future to regional economies in transition—in coal country and elsewhere across the nation. And we need our leaders to stop telling coal miners disheartening fables about days gone by and start telling them the far more promising truth: they have valuable skills, and we need them to help build the clean energy economy of tomorrow.

In fact, that is exactly what's happening in places that are adapting to change and embracing opportunity.

Along the eastern plateau of West Virginia, wind turbines now produce enough electricity to power 125,000 homes. The U.S. Department of Energy's National Renewable Energy Laboratory estimates that West Virginia has the potential to triple its wind generation capacity. And at Eastern West Virginia Community and Technical College, students are learning wind energy turbine technology through degree and certificate programs that lead to good-paying jobs helping to build and service these systems.

The stakes in this are global. Over just the past five years, we've seen $1 trillion invested worldwide in wind and solar power. That market is growing. We need to prepare our workforce for success in this booming market, and the president's Clean Power Plan will help.

A positive approach has been that taken by Kentucky state Representative Harold Rogers, a coal country Republican who worked with Governor Steven Beshear, a Democrat, to hold a bipartisan conference in 2013 on moving the Kentucky economy beyond its heavy dependence on coal. These leaders understand that, even with no limits at all on the carbon pollution coming from coal-fired power plants, Appalachian coal production fell 25 percent between 2006 and 2013, and the Energy Information Administration projects it will fall another 11 percent by 2025.

"Already, Central Appalachian Basin production is fading relentlessly," the *Charleston Gazette* wrote in its June 2014 editorial. "Thick, easy-to-reach seams are nearly depleted, leaving only expensive coal. Lower-priced natural gas and cheap Wyoming coal are grabbing the electricity market. These economic factors are crimping Appalachian coal, regardless of pollution limits."

Up against those forces, "We have no choice but to find additional ways to make a living," Rogers told *The New York Times* in a June 2014 article. That's the kind of leadership we need to create the clean energy solutions of tomorrow—in Kentucky and elsewhere around this country.

PARTNERING WITH CHINA

One of the most peculiar criticisms of those opposed to climate action has come from those who argue that it really won't make any difference because of the growing carbon footprint of China.

Without a doubt, climate change is a global problem no single country can solve by itself. To use China's carbon pollution as an excuse to do nothing about our own, however, is just a way to avoid taking any action at all.

In the first place, it's our responsibility to strike back against the central environmental challenge of our time because it's the right thing to do for our country. We're going to cut our carbon pollution today so our children don't inherit more of the climate chaos that has already begun while needed action is delayed.

We, in the United States, with 4.4 percent of the world's population, account for about 15 percent of the global carbon footprint. That's second only to China, which has 18.9 percent of the world's population and kicks out 27 percent of the world's carbon pollution. On a per capita basis, U.S. carbon emissions are roughly double China's level. And we've contributed more, over time, to the build-up of carbon pollution in our atmosphere than any other country including China.

Let's face it, we've both got work to do. As the two largest sources of global carbon pollution, the United States and China must cooperate to address the growing dangers of climate change. And we're doing it.

NRDC has worked in China since 1996 to advance energy efficiency in its industrial facilities, power plants, and buildings. We opened an office in Beijing in 2006 and have built relationships with Chinese officials, nongovernmental leaders, environmental activists, and entrepreneurs. Our program on environmental governance and open information has helped China strengthen its environmental laws and enforcement capabilities. We helped China to enact its first-ever energy efficiency standards for buildings. Our green supply chain initiative helps to cut carbon emissions and other pollution by calling on multinational corporations to take greater responsibility for the energy and environmental impacts of their factories in China.

President George W. Bush set up the U.S.-China Ten-Year Framework for Energy and Environment Cooperation in 2008, creating a formal mechanism for working together to help advance energy efficiency, improve transportation and power generation systems, and protect air, water, wetlands, and other natural resources. The next year, building on that initiative, President Obama and Chinese President Hu Jintao set up a host of partnerships aimed at fostering innovation in areas like energy efficiency, electric cars, green buildings, smart grid systems and new technology to help capture the carbon emissions from facilities that burn coal. In 2013, the two countries established the U.S.-China Climate Change Working Group to focus on reducing carbon pollution.

"Both sides recognize that, given the latest scientific understanding of accelerating climate change and the urgent need to intensify global efforts to reduce greenhouse gas emissions, forceful, nationally appropriate action by the United States and China—including large scale cooperative action—is more critical than ever," the two countries said in a joint statement in April 2013.

And in the spring of 2014, special U.S. envoy for climate change Todd Stern and his Chinese counterpart, Xie Zhenhua, hosted two days of talks in Washington aimed at coordinating the two countries' policies and advancing the climate change agenda. The meeting was meant to strengthen an enhanced ongoing dialogue between the two countries in the lead-up to United Nations negotiations aimed at inking a global climate change agreement in 2015.

Emerging technologies and innovation have a major role to play, especially when it comes to finding ways to reduce the carbon pollution from burning coal. China burns more coal than any other country on Earth, more, in fact, than the United States, Europe, and Japan combined. China has also become the world's leading investor in a technology called carbon capture and storage, or CCS, which works to capture up to 90 percent of a plant's carbon dioxide emissions before they leave the smokestack, then use that carbon dioxide for industrial processes or bury it in the ground.

The Atlanta-based utility holding company, the Southern Company, is banking on this very technology to capture 65 percent of the carbon emissions from a new coal-fired power plant, giving the plant a lower carbon footprint than most plants that burn natural gas. That will bring the new coal plant well within the new carbon reduction standards the EPA has proposed.

The plant, to open in early 2015 in Mississippi's Kemper County, has supported nearly 12,000 jobs, directly and indirectly, at more than 480 Mississippi companies. It hasn't been cheap. At $5.5 billion, the plant is well over budget. It experienced a litany of problems that led to cost overruns, from bad weather and supplier delays to higher-than-expected costs to install 136 miles of above-ground steel pipe to service the plant.

The Kemper plant, though, is the first of its kind to be built in the United States. Future plants will benefit from lessons learned at Kemper. Costs will come down, as they invariably do when new technologies emerge and are put to use.

To get there, though, we'll need more private investment, and we'll need continued public partnership.

China and the United States are both investing in this new technology to reduce carbon emissions from burning coal. By partnering in this area, as in others, we can both learn from each other.

There's no question that, when the United States leads on issues like climate change, our friends and partners around the world are more eager to work with us, as the chief UN climate official, Christiana Figueres, noted when Obama unveiled his carbon reduction program.

"I fully expect action by the United States to spur others in taking concrete action," she said.

Climate diplomacy is key to addressing this global scourge. Cooperation and policy coordination between the two biggest sources of carbon pollution is vital. Ultimately what matters most, though, is action.

China is the world's largest investor in renewable power, having staked $242 billion in wind, solar, and other types of clean energy generation over just the past five years. That's nearly a third more than the $187 billion in U.S. investment in the sector during that period (2009–2013), according to the United Nations Environment Program, which tracks global investment in renewable energy.

Just since 2007, China has invested more than $500 billion in high-speed rail. More than 100 of its cities are now linked by smooth, modern trains that whisk travelers along at speeds up to 186 miles per hour. Building the system has provided work for scores of thousands of Chinese, from engineers and executives to hammer swingers and shovel bearers. It has improved productivity nationwide, linking technology-rich urban managerial and distribution centers like Shanghai to lower-wage production areas in the hinterlands. And it moves 40 million Chinese each month at a fraction of the carbon footprint of comparable travel by air. Being whisked along China's high-speed rail connections between Beijing and Shanghai, I've become more and more convinced of the need for, and manifest benefits of, investing in this technology in the United States.

And China is investing heavily to make its new buildings and manufacturing facilities more energy efficient. Between 2006 and 2010, the country cut its energy use, as a percentage of overall economic output, by 19 percent. It's on track for an additional 16 percent cut by 2015, in part by making the 10,000 largest energy-using entities in the country subject to mandatory efficiency audits and, where needed, retrofitting to cut down on waste. Through groups like the International Partnership for Energy Efficient Cooperation, China is working to learn energy management practices from countries like the United States, Canada, Japan, France, South Korea, Australia, and others. And China is developing its own technologies and industries around energy-efficient cars, buildings, and factories.

For more than three decades, China's economy has grown at an average rate of close to 10 percent a year, a historic achievement that has lifted half a billion people out of poverty. The growth has come at a high price to the country's environment, because it has been powered largely by dirty energy sources. China is burning as much coal, in fact, as the rest of the world combined. As a result, the country has some of the worst air pollution in the world. Its leaders realize that needs to change. NRDC is working with China's top energy experts to propose a cap on China's national coal consumption. Under the plan, coal use in China would peak in 2020, as the country works to protect its environment, address climate change, and develop its economy.

Meanwhile, it's also important to remember that China expends a lot of its energy—generating a lot of carbon pollution in the process—making products destined for the United States. In the five-year period from 2009–2013, Americans bought a staggering $1.9 trillion worth of goods from China. That's equivalent to our total economic output for a month and a half. If we made those products in the United States, we would use energy, and produce carbon emissions, in doing so. In that sense, we've exported part of our carbon footprint to China. In out-sourcing so much of our pollution to China, we bear some responsibility for helping to clean it up.

It just doesn't do, on any level, for us to point a finger at China and its carbon emissions as justification for failing to act in our country. The stakes are too high for that—at home and abroad. If there's one thing we've learned in confronting other global challenges, it's that U.S. leadership means more abroad when we are prepared to act at home.

Besides carbon pollution, of course, there are other climate-disrupting greenhouse gases—chiefly methane, nitrous oxide and fluorinated gases—that come largely from livestock production, fertilizer use, industrial processes, waste facilities, and the production and distribution of natural gas and oil. Together, these sources add the greenhouse gas equivalent of 1.1 billion tons of carbon pollution to our atmosphere each year. Because they make up 17 percent of our greenhouse gas pollution, these gases, too, must be dramatically reduced as part of an effective strategy to address climate change. Many ranchers and farmers have already begun, improving agricultural land management practices, developing ways to reduce or eliminate the need for tilling the soil and more closely matching fertilization to what crops actually need. Nationally, these efforts are in their infancy. We're just getting started and we've got a long way to go.

SEVEN

Power Forward

In July 2014, the computing and smartphone giant Apple Inc. announced plans to invest $55 million to build a third solar farm to power its massive data center an hour's drive northwest of Charlotte, North Carolina. With two solar panel arrays already providing the data center with enough electricity to power nearly 14,000 homes, the third will increase Apple's total solar output there by 44 percent, using the light of the sun to help power the Cloud.

Three months earlier, General Motors said it would pump $479 million into a pair of Detroit-area facilities, in part to boost production of its Chevy Volt plug-in electric car and the advanced lithium ion batteries that help it to get the equivalent of 98 miles per gallon in a mix of city and highway driving.

And two months before that, fourth-generation rancher Ted Bannister became one of the newest beneficiaries of the national wind turbine boom. He signed on with 16 other landowners across the corn and cattle country of west central Kansas to host a wind farm expected to pay the group some $7.3 million in lease checks over the next 29 years.

"My ancestors and their neighbors pulled sod off the earth to build houses and stone to build fences," Bannister said in a February 2014 statement to news media. "Now we have the chance to produce homegrown electricity from those same winds that blew across my great granddad's field."

From the Sun Belt to the Rust Belt to the Wheat Belt, from some of the youngest corporate leviathans to the oldest names in

111

American commerce and to the boundless fields where men and women still make their living off the land, a 21st century clean-energy revolution is remaking the American economy.

Every day across this country, more than 3.4 million Americans get up, suit up, roll up their sleeves, and go to work helping to create a cleaner and more sustainable future. That figure comes from the U.S. Labor Department's Bureau of Labor Statistics, the most authoritative source anywhere on what's happening in the American workforce.

These are the jobs of tomorrow for workers today: engineers, electricians and roofers; steelworkers, carpenters, tool and die makers; physicists, chemists, and assembly line chiefs. They're building solar panels and wind turbines to power our economy forward with clean and renewable energy. They're weatherizing aging homes so they waste less energy. They're expanding mass transit opportunities, finding new ways to recycle used materials and refuse, and developing the next generation of energy efficient cars, homes, and workplaces.

At a time when our economy is still finding its footing after the worst recession since World War II, these jobs have been a lifeline for millions of families nationwide. In 2013 alone, more than 78,600 new jobs were created just in clean energy and clean transportation at 260 projects. Solar power generation topped the list, as the industry added more than 21,600 workers to install 60 percent more solar capacity than the year before. The jobs, moreover, were spread out all across the country, with California, Texas, Hawaii, Maryland, and Massachusetts among the biggest winners.

Each of those jobs was created by a forward-looking entrepreneur or investor with one eye on the future and the other on the bottom line. As a widening circle of the American business community is discovering every day, creating a cleaner and more sustainable world for future generations is one of the greatest economic opportunities of our lifetime. And it's changing our future—for good.

Hundreds of these business leaders participate in Environmental Entrepreneurs, an NRDC affiliate started in 2000 to bring the business voice to environmental advocacy. E2's 850 members, who range from tech industry CEOs in Silicon Valley to mom and pop solar entrepreneurs in the nation's heartland, know that we can create jobs and spur economic growth by transitioning to clean, renewable energy. They know this through experience: E2's members are involved with 1,700 companies and have created more than

570,000 jobs and control more than $100 billion in venture and private equity funds. They are entrepreneurs like Geoff Chapin, who started Boston-based Next Step Living, which helps people make their homes more energy efficient. In 2012, Next Step was ranked No. 84 on the Inc. 500 list of fastest-growing private companies. They are also people like David Kolsrud, who likes to introduce himself as "an old dirt farmer" from South Dakota. About two decades ago, he began to develop, organize, and fund wind and solar energy projects on farmers and other parts of the Midwest. Today his companies have invested more than $1 billion in renewable energy projects, creating jobs and driving economic growth along the way.

Business leaders like Geoff and David bring an important perspective to the national conversation about energy policy. They are the most nonpartisan group you could encounter—they are simply committed to creating clean energy jobs and calling on elected officials to advance clean energy policies. I have walked the halls of Congress with members of E2 and noticed legislators are very eager to talk with businesspeople who can say: "The clean energy economy is already here, it's employing thousands of your constituents, and it will only grow stronger with the right policies."

Lawmakers are hearing similar messages from American workers. That's what they said at a 2009 labor rally I attended in Gary, Indiana, where we talked about ways clean energy is benefiting homegrown manufacturing. Former EPA administrator Lisa Jackson captured the audience, but Tom Conway, the international vice president of the United Steelworkers, really lit up the room. "This is about jobs, jobs, jobs," he said. "And this is about leaving a clean environment for our kids." The United Steelworkers Union is a partner in the Blue Green Alliance, a collaboration between 15 of the nation's largest union and environmental groups that represents 16 million supporters. Dave Foster, who led the alliance until recently, has been an impassioned advocate for clean energy policies because he has seen them create hundreds of thousands of good-paying jobs around the country.

The fossil fuel industry would have us believe we can't power a modern, industrialized society without oil, gas, and coal. In fact, people across the nation—from E2 members to the steelworkers who build wind turbines—are proving that the shift to clean power is not only possible but inevitable. "These industries are providing real world solutions for reducing emissions of harmful carbon pollution and slowing the effects of climate change," states a September

2013 report from the U.S. Department of Energy that pretty much says it all in its title: *Revolution Now.* "The historic shift to a cleaner, more domestic and more secure energy future is not some far away goal," the report concludes. "We are living it, and it is gaining force."

A BRIGHTER IDEA

What was one of the first household safety lessons we all learned as children? Don't put your finger on a hot light bulb. Since Thomas Edison invented them a century ago, incandescent bulbs have created light by heating a tungsten filament to more than 4,000 degrees Fahrenheit. The light is, in essence, a by-product: 90 percent of the electricity is wasted heating the filament. That never really made much sense, especially each month when the light bill showed up in the mail. But our choices were pretty much that or candlelight.

Now there's a better way. After working for more than a decade to find an efficient replacement for Edison's bulb, the industry—with extensive support from the U.S. Energy Department—has touched the light bulb holy grail. New bulbs that use something called light emitting diodes, or LEDs, have turned the lighting equation on its head. You can replace a 60-watt incandescent bulb with an LED bulb that draws just 9 watts: 85 percent less electricity. That's like paying your electric company a dollar and getting back 85 cents in change. Put another way, it's like cutting the carbon footprint of your lamp down to 15 percent of its current size.

You may have heard that these bulbs are expensive and, at first, they were. The prices, though, have plunged. By August 2014, a top-rated 60-watt equivalent soft-white LED bulb was selling at Home Depot for less than seven dollars. But here's the key: LED bulbs can last up to 25 years. A mom who installs one the year her baby is born will still be enjoying that same bulb when the child graduates from college. And it will have saved her $140 in electricity bills over that time—enough for a graduation present.

Nationally, the potential for savings is huge. The Energy Department estimates there are some four billion screw-in light bulbs in American homes. Lighting, overall, accounts for about 20 percent of our electrical use—commercial, residential, and industrial—nationwide. By 2030, LED lighting will save Americans more than $30 billion a year in electricity costs and cut U.S. energy use for lighting in half, according to the DOE's Office of Energy Efficiency and Renewable Energy.

"This will mean big reductions in carbon pollution, lower energy bills and a more secure energy future for America," the DOE reports.

These new bulbs symbolize the extraordinary benefits to be had in investing in efficiency more broadly. When we add up all the innovations in efficiency—from household dishwashers to commercial heating and cooling systems—the gains have been enormous. In the past four decades, efficiency has done more to meet growing energy needs than oil, gas, and nuclear *combined*, according to the Bipartisan Policy Center. Americans have found so many ways to save energy that we have more than doubled the amount of economic productivity we get out of the oil and electricity we do use. Meanwhile, efficiency is saving our families and businesses scores of billions of dollars each year and helping to make our workers and products more competitive at home and abroad.

For more than 30 years, NRDC has made advocating for efficiency the centerpiece of our energy strategy. Guided throughout this period by attorney Ralph Cavanaugh and physicist David Goldstein, NRDC's team of experts embrace efficiency as the cheapest, cleanest and most abundant energy supply we have in the United States. Our team has helped to design incentives and performance standards that have made our appliances, buildings, factories, and utilities significantly more efficient. NRDC pioneered many of these programs in California, and as a result, the average Californian uses 40 percent less electricity than a typical American. As a result, California residents and businesses have saved more than $65 billion over the past several decades.

And yet, we know we've only scratched the surface. Going forward, the most effective way to reduce our reliance on dirty fossil fuels and the carbon pollution driving climate chaos is to invest in ways to do more with less waste. From the washing machines and air conditioners we use at home to the way we light our shopping malls, heat our offices, and power our industries, American innovation is leading the way to a large and growing range of options for cutting down on energy waste.

No one knows the upper limit of how much we can save, or how new technologies can present emerging opportunities we can't begin to fathom. One thing's for certain: an economy that is spending $1.34 trillion a year on oil, gas, and coal has a lot to gain by cutting waste. How does putting $268 billion a year back in the pockets of our families sound? That's what would happen if we'd cut energy consumption by just 20 percent—and we can do it, over time.

A study by the international consulting firm McKinsey & Company, in fact, found that we could cut our nontransportation energy 23 percent by 2020, savings that would reduce the U.S. carbon footprint by as much as we could from parking—permanently—every car and light truck in America.

We're not likely to park those cars anytime soon, but we're making them more efficient. And more and more of us are discovering the joy of waving out the window and breezing past by the gas station in a hybrid, all-electric, or high-mileage car. Now that we finally have those options, millions of drivers are choosing to save. Some of the most enthusiastic supporters are the taxi drivers I have talked to from Washington, D.C., to Madrid, who love hybrids because they save them money and get up to three times the mileage per gallon of their previous cabs.

54.5 MILES PER GALLON

In 1990, the average American car on the road got 20.2 miles per gallon of gasoline. By 2012, more than two decades later, that figure had risen to just 23.3 miles per gallon. In the quest to get more miles per gallon of gas—and cut tailpipe carbon emissions in the process—we essentially squandered 20 years.

President Obama moved to change that, striking two progressive accords with automakers, the U.S. Environmental Protection Agency, and the U.S. Department of Transportation. The result: automobile fuel efficiency will rise to the equivalent of 54.5 miles per gallon by 2025. Over just 13 years, we'll double the gas mileage of our new automobiles and cut their carbon pollution, per mile driven, in half.

By 2025, that's going to save American consumers, on average, $8,000 at the pump over the life of their car. It will reduce our national oil consumption by more than two million barrels per day. And it will put $336 million back in consumers' pockets every day, assuming gas prices of $4 a gallon.

General Motors, Ford, Chrysler, Toyota, Honda, Nissan, and seven other automakers, which together account for 90 percent of the cars sold in this country, were all on board, and little wonder why. In a 2012 survey conducted by *Consumer Reports*, 37 percent of respondents said fuel efficiency was their number-one consideration in the purchase of a new car.

Finally, consumers looking to get more out of a gallon of gasoline have real options, as automakers work to provide vehicles that shed extra pounds, use advanced technologies that shut engines down when drivers stop for traffic lights, or shut part of the engine down after a car reaches cruising speed on the highway. And, increasingly, Americans are looking to the promise of even greater fuel efficiency, with hybrid and even all-electric cars.

From 2004 to mid-2014, Americans bought more than 3.5 million hybrid cars, which run on electric motors supplemented by traditional gasoline-powered internal combustion engines. Toyota's Prius remains the most popular, accounting for 45 percent of all hybrid sales in July 2014. By then, though, U.S. auto buyers could choose from more than three dozen other hybrid models, including a Honda Accord, Chevy Impala, and Porsche Cayenne. In combined highway and city driving, a hybrid family sedan typically gets anywhere between 42 miles per gallon for, say, a Ford Fusion, to 50 miles per gallon for the Prius, according to EPA ratings.

There are three reasons for the high mileage. First, electric motors are far more efficient than internal combustion engines, which waste about 70 percent of the energy they consume just to operate the machinery itself. Second, electric motors shut off at stop signs and red lights, while gasoline engines waste gas idling. Add to those losses the friction of drive trains, wheels, and tires, and only about two gallons out of every ten of gasoline we put in our cars actually move the vehicle forward. Finally, hybrids use advanced energy-capturing technologies like regenerative brakes, which help to recharge the battery when the car is braking or rolling downhill. That energy is lost in a traditional car.

For many Americans, the beauty of a hybrid is that it recharges itself when the gasoline engine is running. That means they can be driven without stopping to recharge. Drivers who use an all-electric car can get even greater efficiency. Punchy little all-electric cars like the Nissan Leaf, Chevy Spark EV, Honda Fit EV, and Fiat 500e all get the equivalent of more than 100 miles per gallon. To put those savings in perspective, assuming an electricity rate of 12 cents per kilowatt-hour to recharge, the Nissan Leaf can go 1,000 miles on $36 worth of juice.

All-electric cars work best for drivers in urban areas or those with a daily commute of something less than, say, 80 miles, which is how far a car like the Spark can go without recharging the battery. The Chevy Volt is a plug-in electric car that has its own gasoline-powered generator to extend battery range. The electric motor takes the car up to 38 miles on battery power only, then the engine-powered generator kicks in to extend the range to ten times that distance.

All told, Americans bought nearly 600,000 hybrids, plug-in hybrids, and all-electric cars in 2013, accounting for just under 4 percent of U.S. auto sales, according to the Electric Drive Transportation Association, an industry trade group. For the far larger internal combustion car market, higher-mileage options are also on the rise.

We've known for a long time how to get more miles per gallon out of our cars. As far back as 1986, the spunky little Chevy Sprint got 44 miles per gallon, combined city and highway driving. The industry, though, largely took a long holiday from producing fuel-efficient cars. Now they're beginning to return to showrooms, where, even among family-size sedans like the Hyundai Elantra and the Buick Regal, combined fuel efficiency in the 30-miles-per-gallon range is fast becoming the norm. And a growing number of cars, including the Chevy Cruze and Volkswagen Beetle, are being offered with diesel engines that are getting around 33 miles per gallon.

What it all means is that, in the auto industry, we're seeing a revolution in terms of choice, and the potential for saving energy and cutting carbon is enormous. The revolution is benefiting automakers just as much as it is drivers. Just a few years ago, our leading automobile companies were on the brink of collapse, but demand for efficient cars played a key role in their rebound, according to industry analysts. Companies are reinventing themselves and rehiring workers and helping take our country down the path to lower emissions and greater efficiency.

There may be no one who understands the opportunities this presents better than the executive chairman of the Ford Motor Company, William Clay Ford Jr. A lifetime environmentalist, Ford addressed a 2012 meeting of the NRDC board of directors with a message that evoked the can-do spirit of American enterprise. We can remake the entire auto industry, he told us, around a fleet of some of the most efficient cars anywhere in the world, electric cars included. Ford should know. His great-grandfather, Henry Ford, built the beginnings of the American automobile industry from scratch. Skeptics and pessimists abounded. Ford knew, though, that American industry and American workers could build the best automobiles in the world, and he wasn't about to let anyone tell him we couldn't.

Bill Ford is right, too, and the stakes for the country are high.

We burn three hundred and seventy million gallons of gasoline every day in our cars and trucks. At $3.50 per gallon, the tab for the national daily fill up comes to $1.3 billion. By improving our fuel efficiency by just 20 percent—the equivalent of squeezing another five miles out of a gallon of gas—we can put $260 million back into our pockets every single day, while reducing our carbon footprint per mile driven by one-fifth. That's the kind of progress that counts. And we're moving forward to seize it.

"THAT'S THE GOAL"

A light overnight snow lay melting beneath cloudless skies on a bright February morning in 2014, when President Obama journeyed to the sprawling Safeway Distribution Center in Upper Marlboro, Maryland. From that busy hub, he said, large 18-wheel trucks pick up "everything from Doritos to diapers" and deliver them to Safeway grocery stores across the region. Obama, wearing a dark blue suit, white shirt and tie, stood at a podium on a makeshift stage set up in a maintenance garage, a large, hangar-like building with a corrugated steel roof and cinder block walls. Beside him was a Peterbilt truck, a map of the United States emblazoned across its side in red, white and blue.

"U.S. Department of Energy: 10.7 MPG," was written on the truck.

"That's the goal," explained Lenzo Young, a veteran over-the-road driver who stood beaming in the crowd of Safeway employees, trucking executives and others jammed into the garage to hear the president. Young, 60, was wearing a Safeway jacket that read "35 Years of Safe Driving." The jacket, though, was seven years old.

Young explained that each driver's fuel use was closely monitored and posted on a chart each week. A top driver like Tom Jackson—the perennial winner of the depot's annual truck rodeo—averages as much as 6.8 miles per gallon of diesel fuel in one of the big trucks. Most don't do quite that well. If a driver falls below six miles per gallon, though, it signals a problem - for Safeway, and for the country.

These 18-wheel tractor trailers and other heavy-duty trucks account for only 4 percent of the vehicular traffic on our nation's highways. They consume, though, 20 percent of vehicular fuel and account for a comparable amount of the carbon pollution from our vehicles. We're all in this together, moreover, because the big rigs haul 70 percent of the products we use, from fresh tomatoes to radial tires. As long as we depend so heavily on these trucks, we need to make them as efficient as we can.

"That's why we're investing in research to get more fuel economy gains," Obama told the crowd assembled in the garage. Through improvements in aerodynamic design to the tractors and trailers that make up these rigs, advanced engine technologies, more efficient tires, and other innovations, the demonstration Peterbilt truck on display that day had improved its fuel efficiency by 75 percent. "That's why we call this 'Super Truck,'" he said.

In 2011, the EPA, U.S. Department of Transportation, the trucking industry, the state of California and NRDC and others in the environmental community joined hands to create the first-ever national standards for big rig fuel efficiency. The standards are aimed at cutting fuel use per mile by about 20 percent. The move means savings of up to four gallons of diesel fuel for every 100 miles traveled. Combined with similar improvements in fuel efficiency for large pickup trucks, vans, delivery vehicles, and buses, these standards were projected to save vehicle owners and operators a staggering $50 billion in fuel costs over the life of trucks built between 2014 and 2018.

At the Safeway trucking event, Obama directed the EPA and Transportation Department to build on that progress by putting in place, by 2016, the next round of standards for trucks built well into the next decade. The goal is to cut fuel use even further through a combination of engine and transmission efficiency improvements, weight reduction, mechanisms to reduce engine idling time, and improvements in power accessories like air conditioning, water pumps, fans, and other innovations.

In addition to the standards, Obama launched the public-private National Clean Fleets Partnership, which groups two dozen large companies—including Coca-Cola, AT&T, UPS, Staples, and others—in trying to expand the use of alternative fuels, electric vehicles, and other measures aimed at reducing the nation's reliance on oil. Together the members of this partnership operate more than one million commercial vehicles nationwide.

CATCH THE WIND

In 2005, I traveled to Denmark with NRDC colleagues Ashok Gupta, Kit Kennedy, and Sarah Chasis to visit one of the largest offshore wind farms in Denmark, a nation that generates 28 percent of its electricity from wind power. One morning we boarded a boat from the tourist town of Nysted, and at first a summer haze made it hard to see the 72 turbines from shore. But as we drew closer, the white towers appeared in an arc of gleaming white lines. With the quiet hum of these turbines, Denmark taps into a free and inexhaustible resource and generates enough electricity to supply 145,000 homes—all while producing zero climate change pollution.

When we returned to shore, we spoke with Nysted's mayor who told us that at first residents of this popular beach town were deeply concerned about the wind farm. They didn't want it to jeopardize the local tourism industry. Now, the mayor said, they look back and wonder what they were so worried about. Life goes on much as it did before the wind farm, with visitors still drawn to the active harbor for recreational boating.

It was inspiring to hear how this climate solution had become a part of daily life, but I remember wishing I didn't have to travel so far to do it. Today I can see these solutions much closer to home. While America is still moving slowly on offshore projects, we are beginning to embrace the potential of onshore wind power. In the process, we are generating pollution-free power, creating jobs, and providing opportunities for families across the nation.

Farmers in America's heartland are among those benefitting from the wind power surge. The drought and extreme heat of 2012 hit Kansas farmers and ranchers hard, with the Federal Crop Insurance Program paying out $1.3 billion in crop losses in that state alone. For Joe Jury and many of his neighbors near the west Kansas town of Ingalls, it was the worst his family had seen since his great-grandparents weathered the Dust Bowl eight decades before. That made him all the happier to receive $18,000 that year for allowing nine small wind turbines to operate on his wheat and silage fields, part of the $8 million in annual payments to Kansas farmers, ranchers, and others who lease their land to produce electricity from the wind.

"It's there to use as you need it, when you need it, and, in years like this, to use it to make up for the crop income that doesn't come in," he said. "It's kind of like a rainy day fund," he said. "It's Just additional income that helps you when things are short."

Windmills have long been a mainstay across much of the American West, used for generations to help pump water from wells beneath ranches and farms. Over the past decade, though, these romantic-looking throwbacks to the homestead era stand small and spindly in the shadow of modern wind turbines like those rising above the old Jury place. No less than in days gone by, these modern wind turbines are helping to keep the family ranch and farm intact in the face of growing economic pressures. And, much as their lower-tech predecessors once helped to water the fields, today's wind turbines are pumping up the national economy with a growing share of power that's safe, clean, and will never run dry.

"It's truly a blessing for us," explained Powhatan Carter, who gets $35,000 a year for electricity produced from seven wind turbines on the cattle farm his family has operated since 1937. "It's kind of like the sky falls with a little more rain."

Across the Great Plains, and across the country, wind energy is creating jobs, generating income, reducing carbon pollution, and contributing a growing portion of the nation's electricity.

In the first half of 2014, wind turbines generated 5.2 percent of the nation's electricity—a record, and up from 1.3 percent just six years before—with enough capacity to power nearly 16 million average American homes, according to the American Wind Energy Association.

Iowa got 27 percent of its electricity from wind turbines in 2013, while it generated 19 percent of the electricity in Kansas. Texas, the oil capital of the world, got 10 percent of its electricity in 2013 from the wind. By early 2014, the Lone Star State had enough wind turbines in place to power 3.3 million average American homes, and it had enough new turbines under construction to increase the states capacity by another 60 percent.

By 2030, the Department of Energy has said, wind turbines could provide 20 percent of the nation's electricity, roughly what the nuclear power industry provides us with now—and we're quickly moving ahead. As wind turbine efficiency improves, costs have fallen. New wind turbines will produce electricity for about 16 percent less than coal, an April 2014 study by the Energy Information Administration showed.

SUNNY AND BRIGHT

Apple's growing investment near Charlotte is part of a solar boom. In the first half of 2014, the industry installed nearly 40 percent more solar panels than the year before, and nearly double the level of 2012. As of August 2014, there were enough solar panels operating nationwide to power three million typical American homes, the Solar Energy Industries Association reported.

Together, solar and wind accounted for 44 percent of all the new electricity-generating capacity in the United States during 2012 and 2013. These are actual generating capacity figures from the Federal Energy Regulatory Commission, which oversees U.S. electricity generation and reliability. In that same time, we got 37 percent of our new generation capacity from natural gas and 14 percent from coal.

The shift toward more wind and solar power has been good news for the American economy, where nearly 200,000 workers are now designing, building, and maintaining wind and solar power systems. And certainly the shift is good for the environment and public health. All of that has economic benefits, as the public has clearly recognized.

Kansas, Ohio, North Carolina, Missouri, and 24 other states, for instance, are promoting wind, solar, and other forms of renewable power through policies that are creating jobs and generating investment. By establishing renewable portfolio standards, these states call on utilities to generate or purchase a certain percentage of their power through renewable sources like wind turbines. In most cases, the target ranges from 10 percent to 25 percent by the year 2025. Six of these states—Hawaii, California, Colorado, Minnesota, Connecticut, and Oregon—expect to get 25 percent, or more, of their power from renewable sources.

The standards that promoted this progress are under threat from none other than the fossil fuel industry. The effort is being spearheaded by a group called the American Legislative Exchange Council, or ALEC. It is funded by a collection of Tea Party backers and corporate giants including ExxonMobil, Peabody Energy (the largest private coal company in the world), and Charles Koch, chairman and chief executive officer of Koch Industries, and his brother, David Koch, the company's executive vice president. ALEC is connected to more than 35 "model bills" to roll back renewable energy standards in statehouses across the country. Thus far, every effort has failed because people see the value in fostering a local clean energy sector. Kansas and North Carolina both beat back attempts to repeal their renewable power standard, in part because the programs had generated more than 10,000 local jobs in each of those states.

In expanding our use of wind and solar power at home, we're building a beachhead for success in a rapidly growing global market.

In the five years from 2009 to 2013, global investment in renewable energy totaled more than $1.1 trillion. Of that, $992 billion—87 percent—was for electricity generation from the wind and the sun, according to the United Nations Environmental Program, which tracks this investment. Europe accounts for nearly half the total investment. China invested $242 billion during the five-year period, nearly one-third more than the United States at $187 billion. Nationally, China is the world's largest investor in renewable power. Whether traveling across Europe or across China, you can see the transformation of renewable energy being deployed across the world.

Globally, wind, solar, biomass, and other forms of renewable energy have accounted for 44 percent of all new electricity-generating capacity worldwide during 2012 and 2013, Bloomberg reports, cutting annual global carbon pollution by 1.2 billion tons. And the International Energy Agency estimates that wind, solar, and other sources of renewable power will account for nearly half of all new power generation worldwide between now and 2035. By then, the group predicts, more than 30 percent of global electricity will come from renewable sources, rivaling coal as the world's largest source of electricity.

THE NEXT GLOBAL ENERGY SUPERPOWER

From the heyday of coal and steam two centuries ago, to the era of oil and gas, the United States has been an energy superpower. We've also led the world in technology and productivity. Our future will build on our strengths and success, but it will be shaped by the decisions we make today about the kind of country we want to become tomorrow. We can cling by our fingernails to the fossil fuels of the past and consign future generations to all the damage and cost and risk that entails. Or, we can combine our strengths as an energy, technology, and productivity dynamo to strengthen and broaden the clean energy revolution we've already begun. Much of the country has made up its mind. Investors are betting scores of billions of dollars a year on commonsense innovations that are moving us beyond our reliance on fossil fuels and passing on to our children the opportunity to lead the world into a new era of safer, more sustainable, renewable power.

At the dawn of each revolution that has shaped this country, there have been those who strained to grasp what people of vision saw clearly. There have been those who squinted out toward the horizon unable to imagine what lay beyond. And there have been those who felt that the way things were was good enough, and making things better wasn't worth the risk.

The people who built this country, though, the people who have given it strength, have always been the people of vision, the people of courage, the people who were driven to ride out onto the frontier, seize the future and make it their own. That spirit of endeavor, of striving, of insisting on being better tomorrow than we are today, that is what has guided this nation forward since our founding. That is what must guide us still.

On his Grammy-winning 1996 album, *Unchained*, the late Johnny Cash covered Rusty Cage, songwriter Chris Cornell's stark vision of human struggle in the shadows of an American wasteland. "I'm burning diesel, burning dinosaur bones," Cash sings, later vowing in his gravely baritone, "I'm gonna' break my rusty cage."

I won't pretend to get into the mind of either artist. When I hear the song, though, it conjures up a future made bleak by our addiction to fossil fuels, a nightmare redeemed by one man's defiant pledge to break free of the destructive ways of the past. It's time we all mustered the defiance to turn away from our costly dependence on dangerous and dirty fuels. It's time we set American innovation and opportunity free. It's time to break that rusty cage.

EIGHT

Standing Vigil, Running Strong

Manny Diaz was seven the year he and his mother fled Castro's Cuba for Miami, reenacting a human drama that has reinvigorated our country, one determined immigrant at a time, from its beginnings. Growing up amid the colorful shops and bustling sidewalks of Little Havana, he played baseball year round at local parks, went to family barbecues on the outskirts of town and swam with his friends in the ocean.

"Mom would make a ham sandwich, that she'd cut in two, and a Coke, and we'd go hang out at the beach all day," he recalled to several of my NRDC colleagues and me in 2014. Folks with money, he said, might go to restaurants or movies, "but, when you can't afford it, it's you and nature."

Diaz never forgot that lesson, or the example his mother set by embracing opportunity with both hands, even when it meant traveling an uncertain course.

And so, when he was elected mayor of Miami in 2000, Diaz moved with a determination all his own to restore the natural systems of the city he loved. Over the next eight years, he turned around a long history of environmental degradation, cleaned up parks and waterways, established bike lane,s and cut energy waste in city buildings, facilities and schools. He initiated one of the most assertive sustainability programs anywhere in the country, including a "Green Lab" to help promote energy efficient building design.

Diaz was one of the first mayors to sign on to the U.S. Conference of Mayors' Climate Protection Agreement. Initiated in 2005 by

Seattle Mayor Greg Nickels, the pact has been signed by more than 1,060 mayors, representing 90 million people in Cleveland, Atlanta, Milwaukee, Boston, and other cities in all 50 states. The signatories have vowed to reduce carbon emissions in their cities below 1990 levels, through actions ranging from land use policies that discourage sprawl to urban forest restoration projects. They have also pledged to urge state and federal governments to enact policies and programs to cut carbon pollution nationally, and to urge Congress to pass bipartisan greenhouse gas reduction legislation.

"Mayors are already on board," said Diaz, a former president of the mayors' conference. "The mayors said, 'We're not going to sit back and wait for those idiots in Washington to figure this out' — you can quote me on that — 'We're going to do it ourselves.'"

A WIDENING CONSENSUS FOR CHANGE

Across the country, widening and increasingly diverse groups of Americans are taking action to create a more sustainable world. As our gridlocked Congress fails to act, leaders of communities large and small are moving ahead, starting in their own backyards. Close to home and far afield, they're making an important difference, cutting our carbon footprint and strengthening the momentum for even greater progress to come. Politicians at the national level may be divided along partisan lines over whether we power our country into the 21st century with the clean energy of tomorrow or anchor our future to the dirty fuels of the past. Increasingly, though, that artificial and counterproductive political divide is being left behind by a powerful national consensus for change.

More than seven Americans in ten understand that climate change is a threat, a June 2014 Bloomberg National Poll found. And an *NBC News/Wall Street Journal* poll found that 67 percent of Americans support the plan President Obama announced in the same month to limit the carbon pollution from our power plants. From state to state, they're standing up to say so. In eight days of summer hearings on the plan in Atlanta, Denver, Pittsburg, and Washington, nearly 1,300 people got to address Environmental Protection Agency officials, and more than 1,100 of those spoke out for strong EPA action to address climate change.

If you're imagining these advocates as backpack-toting granola crunchers, think again. The people who took time from busy schedules, families, and jobs to stand up for a more sustainable future included scientists and lawyers, working moms and dads, farmers and ranchers, investors, teachers, retirees, and entrepreneurs. People who understand the threat of climate change are as likely to be wearing wing tips and heels as Birkenstocks. And the voices calling for action form an American chorus as rich with the strains of hip hop, hymns, and salsa as with folk ballads and rock 'n roll.

Whether through the influx of immigrant talent and drive, the values and traditions of native peoples, families whose roots reach several generations deep, or the essential ongoing replenishment of our nation's youth, our country is changing, and our movement is changing with it. We're working to connect the dots between the environmental agenda and the lives of women, Millennials, people of color, corporate executives, organized labor, Latinos, outdoorsmen, faith-based communities and other groups. There's more to this than merely growing our base. We're far more effective when we're able to tap into a talent pool that reflects who we are as a nation, our diverse backgrounds, perspectives and strengths. That's always been true, and never more so than now, as we confront a challenge as complex as our nation is varied.

Climate change is an issue for all Americans. Its impacts are affecting us everywhere. And some of its worst damage and greatest risk hits first and hardest against people of color, low-income communities, and minorities of all types.

"Global climate change has a disproportionate impact on communities of color in the United States and around the world," the nation's oldest civil rights group, the National Association for the Advancement of Colored People (NAACP), states on its website. The NAACP established its Climate Justice Initiative, the site states, "to educate and mobilize communities to address this human and civil rights issue."

African Americans, Latinos, Native Americans, and other minorities increasingly, and disproportionately, find themselves in the path of climate chaos. The link between minority status and income means that these communities are more likely to live near a coal-fired power plant or incinerator than the population at large. They're exposed to greater levels of the kinds of air pollution that increase asthma attacks and other respiratory ills, especially among children and seniors. They're more likely to live in the inner city, where neighborhoods are significantly hotter in summer than non-urban areas, and they have higher rates of heat-related illness and death than non-Hispanic white populations, the NAACP reports. Minority groups tend to live disproportionately in lower-lying areas that are subject to flooding. And in places like southern Louisiana, rising sea levels are swallowing up entire communities, forcing families to abandon land their ancestors have worked for generations and breaking up traditional cultures and ways of life. Ben Jealous, the former chief executive officer of the NAACP, met with me and other national environmental leaders in 2014 to talk about the need for our communities to join together and make climate justice a part of the broader civil rights agenda.

"For so many of these people, environmental protection is about daily life," said Adrianna Quintero, NRDC director of Latino Outreach. "What's in the air I'm breathing? Is it safe for my kids to drink the water?" Adrianna has worked for more than 15 years engaging Latinos in environmental advocacy, from educating farm workers about the health risk of pesticides to helping launch Voces Verdes, a group of Latino business executives who support clean energy. Together with Al Huang, NRDC's lead environmental justice litigator, Adrianna is helping communities threatened by climate change and fossil fuel development. "We're all part of the solution, no matter what language we speak." Adriana believes. "I've learned from listening to people's questions and stories about the urgent need for change."

The urgency comes from being on the front lines.

"People of color care deeply about the environment and the impacts of climate change," said Nikki Silvestri, executive director of Green for All, a non-profit group that advocates for the power of a green economy to lift low-income families out of poverty. "We understand the urgency of these threats," she said in a July 2014 statement, "because we experience the effects every single day."

Some African American leaders talk about climate change, in fact, as the next great barrier for people of color to overcome, drawing inspiration from those who marched for civil rights five decades ago.

"While they were fighting for equality, we are fighting for existence," the Rev. Lennox Yearwood told an estimated 35,000 people gathered near the Washington Monument in the nation's capital on a bitter cold day in February 2013 for "Forward on Climate." Yearwood is president of the Hip Hop Caucus, a movement that focuses on social and political progress for African Americans. In a reference to the lunch counter sit-ins that spotlighted racial injustice generations ago, Yearwood has said standing up to the dangers of climate change and the promise of clean energy is "our lunch-counter moment for the 21st century."

"I'M STANDING UP FOR JUSTICE"

It's a moment, also, for a new generation of American stewards who see issues of environmental protection as a straightforward marriage of moral obligation and common sense.

"I'm standing up for justice, and it's through a frame related to the environment," explains Rob Friedman, an NRDC staff member who started campaigning for clean energy while he was still in high school and now helps mobilize other young people for climate action. "The things that we're fighting for are basic human rights in a lot of ways," he said. "These are normal things to be fighting for . . . it's about justice."

And that means it's about people.

"I studied sustainable development in college," adds 23-year-old Chelsea Phipps, who joined NRDC's staff shortly after graduating and researching water issues in New Delhi. "I worked on water, that was my main issue, and I had always looked at it through the human lens." And that's what drives her still.

I remember what it meant to my generation to stand up and speak our minds—about women's rights, Vietnam, and civil rights. Today's youth is no different, whether they're taking to the streets for rallies like the Forward on Climate rally or getting out the vote for candidates who support climate action. And, as in my day, many young activists are emerging from college campuses. People like Billy Parrish, who came to talk with me when he was a sophomore at Yale University. He had started a network of students groups called Energy Action Coalition to push campuses to reduce carbon pollution and urge lawmakers to support clean energy and climate solutions. The network Billy helped create became so successful, he dropped out of college and devoted himself full time to the campaign, traveling from school to school, sleeping on couches, and mobilizing young people along the way. Today, Energy Action Coalition is one of the largest youth organizations dedicated to climate action. And Billy recently founded Mosaic, Inc., a company that enables crowd-funding of community solar projects from the Navajo Nation to Oakland to West Virginia.

Energy Action Coalition helped launch the Power Shift summits, which gather thousands of young activists every year to demand climate justice, divest from fossil fuels, fight fracking, and build a clean energy economy. The summits often include a day of lobbying on Capitol Hill and training sessions in lobbying, canvassing, nonviolent direct action, and other forms of advocacy. That is a level of sophistication most of my peers simply didn't have in our college days.

This generation of activists is gathering the tools they need to build political influence and strengthen the consensus for change. They work at the local level, and they get support from national networks like Bill McKibben's brilliant youth-oriented group, 350.org. Bill is good friend and a constant source of inspiration for me. He communicates powerfully about our moral obligation to address climate change and end our fossil fuel addiction. But words are not enough for Bill. He takes action, and he galvanizes others to do the same. Working on a shoestring budget, Bill has used personal leadership, potent prose, and the global reach of the Internet to connect a largely under-thirty crowd to the vital issues of dirty fuels, climate change, and clean energy. His organization takes its name from the goal of reducing world atmospheric carbon dioxide concentrations to 350 parts per million, down from 400 parts per million as of mid-2014 by reducing our reliance on fossil fuels, to stabilize global climate.

I spoke at one of the very first 350.org actions at the Museum of the American Indian in Washington, D.C., and I remember the energized crowd of young faces; Bill had clearly tapped into a powerful vein of committed action. The organization's reach has spread like wildfire since then, thanks to the tireless dedication of Bill and 350.org executive director May Boeve.

Bill, May, and others have combined to help lead the youth-driven effort to get colleges and universities to help advance a cleaner energy future in two ways: first, by reducing their own carbon footprint by investing in energy efficiency, renewable power, and other sustainability measures; and second by stripping fossil fuel companies out of the investment portfolios in their endowments. The amounts of these endowments are huge, totaling $449 billion in 2013 for the 835 colleges and universities tracked by the National Association of College and University Business Owners.

Young activists are pushing for divestment from existing fossil fuel projects, and they are calling for an end to dangerous proposals like the Keystone XL pipeline for tar sands oil. These young people realize that building a massive piece of infrastructure for some of the dirtiest fuel on earth will lock their generation into decades of oil dependence and climate change pollution. Like the tens of thousands of Americans already living on the front lines of fossil fuel development—from the oil-soiled shores of the Gulf of Mexico to the fracking fields of Colorado to the mine-scarred hillsides of West

Virginia—young people are standing up for a better future. They support an energy system that does not put their health and families at risk. And they are making their voices heard in local communities, at anti-Keystone XL rallies outside the White House, and in state and national elections.

GROWING THE MOVEMENT

I am deeply inspired by the growing movement for climate action. People are joining together across the nation to create a more sustainable future. This is a promising start, but we need to do more. We need to expand the ranks of the movement even farther. We are locked in a fight with the most powerful industry in the nation. To make ourselves heard above the din of fossil fuel companies, we must raise a louder battle cry.

How do we do that? Over the past several years, NRDC has been working with allies and partner groups to add new voices to the chorus. First and foremost, we try to connect to people's daily lives. More and more, parents who live in big cities or have children with asthma are coming to understand that climate change will lead to increased smog and greater risk of respiratory illness. Small business owners in coastal towns are figuring out the financial costs of managing rising sea levels and storm surges.

Dr. Katherine Hayhoe, a climate scientist at Texas Tech in Lubbock and a devout Christian, appeared in the 2014 Showtime series, *Years of Living Dangerously,* talking to a group of people in Plainview, Texas. The town has been so badly hit by drought that the local Cargill meat packing plant had to close because ranchers couldn't run enough cattle on their parched rangeland to supply the plant. Many residents viewed the drought in terms of natural cycles, but then Dr. Hayhoe explained the mechanics of climate change—and infused her explanation with Christian values. "When I look at the information we get from the planet," she said. "I look at it as God's creation speaking to us. And, in this case, there is no question that God's creation is telling us that it is running a fever." After her talk, an audience member explained why he found it compelling. "When you have somebody that believes the same way as you, has lived here for quite a while and is teaching at Texas Tech, you see that conservative side of that telling you that message. It sure makes a lot of difference."

It makes a difference, also, when people hear about workable solutions, like cleaning up our power plants and investing in efficiency and renewable energy. The fossil fuel industry would have us believe that America can't power a modern, industrialized society without fossil fuel. NRDC and allies prove them wrong. We point to the hundreds of thousands of Americans already working in the clean energy sector, the states already getting sizeable chunks of their energy from renewable power, and the countless towns and cities already reducing their carbon pollution.

We work hard to bring more voices into the climate movement. We do it because we must.

NRDC and our allies have designed countless solutions for reducing carbon pollution and promoting clean energy. We know what policies will help us fight climate change. But in a deeply divided political landscape awash in corporate money, smart solutions alone are not enough. We have to generate the political will to put good ideas in place. We need to create a groundswell of support for climate action.

At nearly every event I attend, people ask me what they can do to address climate change. I encourage them to insulate their homes and use energy efficient appliances. But I make it clear that alone is not enough. I urge them to speak up, write letters to the editor, ask what their mayor is doing on climate change, demand that their lawmakers support climate solutions, tell the EPA they support strong limits on carbon pollution. These actions make a difference. Together, they have helped prevent fossil fuel companies and their allies from rolling back clean energy standards in several states, they have helped pass and defend the first-ever climate change law in California, and they have led to the first-ever plan to cut the dangerous carbon pollution from the power plants that account for 40 percent of our national carbon footprint.

Raising our voices works. That's why wherever I speak—to business groups, city mayors, fracking activists, college students, Garden Club associations—I give the same charge: speak to the people in your community about the threat of climate change and demand action from leaders in local, state, and national government.

I make this request, because when we connect climate change to people's communities, when we help them envision a clean energy future, and when we inspire them to take action, we create something even more powerful than behavioral change. We create citizen engagement—one of the most powerful forces against climate change.

The environmental movement, like the broader movement for social justice and progressive change, is about creating a better world. It's about reaching out to all communities, listening to their stories, hearing their concerns, and connecting to the way environmental threats and costs are affecting them and their families in their daily lives. From the front lines of climate change to the most distant ramparts of our international reach, the message could not be more clear: we must reduce our reliance on fossil fuels and invest in building the clean energy economy of tomorrow.

THE WORLD WE CREATE

There are moments in every country's history when its destiny is affirmed and its greatness renewed by the capacity of its people to rally around a shared goal—some urgent imperative or opportunity—then summon the common resources and collective will required to achieve it. From the moment of our founding, this nation has risen to such moments. That's how we built the railroads and canals that knitted this country together at its birth. It's how we won World War II. It's how we won the Cold War. It's how we put a man on the moon.

Over the course of the next generation, we face no more urgent environmental imperative, and no greater economic opportunity, than to shift to a clean energy future that can break our dependence on fossil fuels, restore U.S. leadership in the global marketplace, and strike a blow against the climate change that threatens us all.

Ultimately we will all understand that these goals are not options, and never were. They're a vital part of the prosperous and secure future we all want to leave to our children. These goals transcend ideology and cross partisan lines. They are so profoundly essential and so thoroughly imbedded in the national interest that to fail to attain them would pose a genuine threat to the way of life we all value and cherish.

We in the environmental movement, the social justice movement, the movement for a more sustainable world, the movement to treat our natural systems as the most important physical asset we share and to care for those systems as if our lives depended upon them, we are embarked, all of us, on the mission of our lifetime. We hold, each of us, in the palm of our hand, more influence than any other people at any other time in any other place in the history of the world. The positions we press, the decisions we make, and the actions we take will determine the fate, not only of our own future, but also of the future of the generations to come. Will we consign them to a world of mounting destruction and waste, a place that grows more devoid of life and more desolate of spirit with each measure of dirty fuel we consume, or will we grant them as our crowning legacy the promise of a brighter tomorrow, a world where the natural systems we depend upon are honored, protected, and cherished, as if we were counting on them for our last breath of air?

I believe we'll affirm our destiny. I believe we'll summon our strength. I believe we'll rise to this challenge, as we have before, stand up, speak out, and be heard. Even when we count our gains in inches, I believe we will stay the course, focus on solutions until by degrees we succeed, certain that there's no turning back to a world that pits the power of the corporate balance sheet against the well being of the planet, its people and all it supports.

I believe in that vision. I've lived it. I've seen it at work. I know how far it's brought us, and I know there's a new generation of environmental champions pushing for even more progress with all the restless urgency, optimism, and faith of a determined people united for change. It won't happen overnight, or in a straight line, or in some grand bargain that can expunge from our future the mistakes of our past. But it must happen over time, and now is the time for us to begin. We have it within us to rally around this great goal and to bend the resources and summon the will to achieve it. That is what we've always done in this country, whenever challenge and opportunity have knocked, not only for ourselves, but for those who will one day inherit and be called on to watch over the world that we create.

Epilogue

CO_2 Zero: Carbon Neutral USA In Our Lifetime

In May 1961, President John F. Kennedy asked the American people to rally around an audacious idea.

"I believe that this nation should commit itself to achieving the goal, before this decade is out, of landing a man on the moon," Kennedy said, "and returning him safely to the earth."

We didn't have the technology to do it. The path ahead was unmarked and unclear. There were plenty who predicted failure and some who doubted we should even try. Over the next eight years, however, we pulled together and got it done, in a national effort unmatched in peacetime that drew on the strengths and talents of hundreds of thousands of Americans from every conceivable walk of life.

Breaking free from our addiction to fossil fuels is the great Apollo mission of our time. The challenges are no less daunting, but the imperative to act is clear. It is time for us, as Americans, to state as a national goal that we will strengthen and accelerate our efforts to clean up our carbon pollution, invest in energy efficiency and shift to renewable power so that, within our lifetime, we will become a carbon-neutral nation that no longer contributes to climate change.

That means we will reduce our reliance on coal, gas, and oil. We will cut our carbon footprint. And we will protect and restore our forests and wetlands so that we offset every pound of carbon pollution we produce by adding to our natural capacity to absorb it.

The objective is clear and achievable. It will focus our priorities and organize our resources around a new vision for our future. It will put millions of Americans to work in good-paying jobs that can't be sent overseas. It will make our companies more competitive, our country more secure, and our children more healthy and prosperous. It will restore American leadership on the global imperative to address climate change. It will strike a powerful blow against the central environmental challenge of our time and help avert global economic and humanitarian catastrophe. And it will send the message to future generations that we will honor our obligation to leave the world in better shape for them than it was left to us.

Those are national stakes worthy of national commitment. United around this goal and the will to see it through, we cannot help but prevail.

A CLEAR AND ACHIEVABLE GOAL

We know how to reduce our carbon footprint, and we've already started to do it. More than 3.4 million Americans are on the job every day helping to clean up our dirty power plants, get more electricity from the wind and sun, and cut energy waste in our homes, at work and on the road.

Through these and other measures we can slash our carbon pollution from 5.4 billion tons in 2013 to 750 million tons by 2050, a July 2014 United Nations study on U.S. energy options found. By 2050, we can get 80 percent of our electricity from renewable sources, concludes a 2012 study by the U.S. National Renewable Energy Laboratory, part of the Department of Energy (DOE). And we can cut gasoline use 80 percent in our cars and light trucks by 2050, according to a 2013 study by the National Academy of Sciences.

We know we can shrink our carbon footprint, in other words, to less than one-fifth its current size by 2050. But we have to act much sooner. Our own history tells us we can, our children's future demands that we must.

By investing in efficiency, we'll do more with less waste. Over the past 35 years, we've cut our energy use in half, as a share of our economic output, saving trillions of dollars. Going forward, we can do even better. Technology and innovation advance over time at an accelerating rate. Progress builds on itself. By getting just 4 percent more efficient each year, we'll cut our energy use 65 percent by 2050, while our economy continues to grow and becomes leaner and more competitive worldwide.

We're going to double the gas mileage of our new-car fleet by 2025, and we need to keep improving. That means raising the efficiency of cars powered by conventional internal combustion engines. And it means putting more hybrid electric cars like the Toyota Prius on the road, along with more plug-in electric cars like the Chevy Volt and all-electric cars like the Ford Focus Electric.

We'll always need energy. We need to communicate, too, but we're not stuck with fax machines and dial tone. There are better ways to power our future than by digging fossil fuels from the ground and setting them on fire. The DOE study envisions renewable energy generating 80 percent of our electricity by mid-century. We have to get there sooner, and it's clear that we can. Two renewable power sources, wind and solar, provided just 1.4 percent of our electricity in 2008. By mid-2014, that figure was 5.5 percent—a fourfold increase in less than six years. No one should doubt we can get most of our electricity from renewable sources—and the sooner we do that, the better.

CARBON FOOTPRINTS IN THE FOREST

Healthy forests and wetlands stand sentry against the dangers of climate change, absorbing carbon dioxide from the atmosphere and locking it away in plants, root systems and soil. About 16 percent of our carbon pollution gets tucked away each year in our public and private forests. We need to do more, though, to protect and strengthen this restorative resource if we expect it to do the same for us.

Forests aren't fuel, and we need to stop mowing them down to make wood pellets to fire generators. They're not the place for reckless exploitation, and we need to stop industrial logging that rips up ancient groves from places like the Tongass National Forest. They're not urban centers, and we need to be smarter about development and stop sacrificing our forests to senseless sprawl. And we need to restore former forests that were cleared long ago for reasons that no longer make sense.

We can offset carbon pollution, also, by taking better care of our nation's wetlands. Mangroves, salt marshes, and sea grass lock away carbon from the atmosphere at up to five times the rate of tropical forests. We can expand our national carbon sponge by protecting existing wetlands and restoring places like coastal Louisiana, where, in less than a century, we've lost enough coastal land to cover the state of Delaware. We cannot stand idle while Louisiana loses a piece of coastal land the size of a football field every hour. Instead, we must help restore wetlands and forests in our pursuit of the larger goal of becoming carbon-neutral in our lifetime. As we work to build the low-carbon economy of the future, these natural systems will help to absorb the carbon pollution we produce—for as long as we still produce it.

No one knows what innovations lie ahead to help stamp out our carbon footprint even sooner than we might yet imagine. This much, though, is certain. We have what it takes to break our costly addiction to fossil fuels and create a clean energy future. We can stand up to strike down the central environmental challenge of our time. We can become carbon-neutral in our lifetime. We must make up our minds to do it then set ourselves on course to succeed in the Apollo mission of our time. Once we do that, no power on Earth can turn us around.

Index

accidents: fracking, 64, 65–66; from
  pipelines, 44. *See also* disasters
Adams, John, 11
Adirondack mountains, 9–10
Adirondack Park, 9–10
Africa, 8–9
air pollution: carbon footprint
  relating to, 97–102; from
  fracking, 54. *See also* carbon
  dioxide; carbon footprint; Clean
  Air Act
Alaska, 26, 38
American Legislative Exchange
  Council (ALEC), 123–124
Andrus, Cecil, 11
Apollo 8, 4
Apple Inc., 111, 122
Arctic Ocean: marine animals in, 36;
  oil in, 35–39; risk in, 38–39; sea
  ice, 87–88
auto industry. *See* cars

backyard fracking, 55–58
Bakken oil, 69–70, 71–73
Bannister, Ted, 111
Bates, Sarah, 7
birds, 41–42
bitumen. *See* oil; tar sands
Black Panthers, 7
Blue Green Alliance, 113
boreal forest, 39–46
Boston Redevelopment Authority, 4
BP Deepwater Horizon disaster:
  aftermath, 25–35; change needed
  after, 31–32; conditions leading
  to, 30–31; on fishing, 28–29;
  lessons from, 31–34; marine

animals affected by, 27–29;
  National Commission on BP
  Deepwater Horizon Oil Spill and
  Offshore Drilling, 29; Obama on,
  29; overview of, 26, 27–29; risk
  after, 34–35; total oil spilled, 27
Bukavu, 8–9
Bureau of Land Management, 60
Bureau of Safety and
  Environmental Enforcement,
  33–34
Bush, George, H.W., 12, 79
Bush, George, W., 59; China relating
  to, 106
Bush Administration, 13

California: climate laws in, 2;
  drought, 77–78; Santa Barbara oil
  well, 5–6
Canada: boreal forest, 39–46;
  Quebec train disaster, 72;
  TransCanada Corporation, 44,
  45; U.S. relating to, 46–47
cancer crisis, 42–43
carbon dioxide: Bush
  Administration on, 13; Clean Air
  Act on, 13; description of, 80;
  from Keystone XL pipeline, 45;
  ocean relating to, 86; rates, 80;
  from tar sands production, 43–46
carbon footprint: air pollution
  relating to, 97–102; of China,
  105–106, 109; Clean Air Act on,
  98–102; Clean Power Plan on,
  93–94; electricity relating to,
  94–95, 95; EPA on, 94, 97; health
  relating to, 97; NRDC on, 95, 134;

About the Authors

Frances Beinecke is president of the Natural Resources Defense Council, the nation's foremost environmental advocacy group, where she has fought to protect our natural systems and public health since 1972.

President Barack Obama named Ms. Beinecke in 2010 to serve on the National Commission on the BP Deepwater Horizon Oil Spill and Offshore Drilling. She serves, or has served on, the board of directors of the World Resources Institute, the Wilderness Society, the New York League of Conservation Voters, the Energy Future Coalition, the China-U.S. Center for Sustainable Development, and Conservation International's Center for Environmental Leadership in Business.

Ms. Beinecke earned her bachelor's degree from Yale College, where she was a member of the first class of women to graduate. She holds a master's degree from the Yale School of Forestry and Environmental Studies. She co-chairs the Leadership Council of the Yale School of Forestry, is a member of the Yale School of Management's Advisory Board, and a former member of the Yale Corporation.

She has received the Rachel Carson Award from the National Audubon Society, the Distinguished Alumni Award from the Yale School of Forestry and Environmental Studies, the Annual Conservation Award from the Adirondack Council, and the Robert Marshall Award from the Wilderness Society.

She is co-author of the 2009 book, *Clean Energy Common Sense: An American Call to Action on Global Climate Change*. Her op-eds have been published by *The New York Times,Los Angeles Times, The Washington Post, The Economist*, and more than a dozen other newspapers and she appears regularly on NPR, MSNBC, PBS *Newshour*, and other nationally broadcast programs.

Ms. Beinecke and her husband Paul have three daughters and live in New York City.

Bob Deans is director of editorial content for the Natural Resources Defense Council, the nation's foremost environmental advocacy group. He spent 25 years as a correspondent for the *Atlanta Journal-Constitution* and other papers in the Cox newspapers chain, including four years as Chief Asia Correspondent, based in Tokyo, and eight years covering the White House. He is a former president of the White House Correspondents' Association.

Deans is the author of the 2012 book, *Reckless: The Political Assault on the American Environment*; the 2007 book, *The River Where America Began: A Journey Along the James*. He is co-author of the 2009 book, *Clean Energy Common Sense: An American Call to Action on Global Climate Change*; and the 2010 book, *In Deep Water: The Anatomy of a Disaster, the Fate of the Gulf and Ending Our Oil Addiction*. He and his wife Karen have three children and live in Bethesda, Maryland.